ASSROOM

IEHL & MELISSA GOODRICH

VAKE

DANA DIEHL & MELISSA GOODRICH

THE CLASSROOM

Published by Gold Wake Press

Cover design by Nick Courtright
nickcourtright.com
Cover image by Andrea Ucini
andreaucini.com

10 9 8 7 6 5 4 3 2 1

The Classroom
2019, Dana Diehl and Melissa Goodrich

goldwake.com

TABLE OF CONTENTS

To our teachers

THE BOY WHO ARRIVES IN A BOX

The CDs arrive with our son. He's in low-power mode when we open the crate, nestled in a bed of packing peanuts. His name, username, and password are affixed to his white cotton T-shirt with a safety-pin. His bangs are long and fall over his closed eyes. There is a glossy parents' manual beneath his head that's at least twice the size of a phone book.

Still, the CDs are what overwhelm me.

The CDs come in by the hundreds. Dozens of boxes piled beside the door. The postman is kind enough to wheel them in our front hallway, where they line up, pile by pile. My husband unpacks our son. "He's skinny," he says, lifting him up carefully so as not to scrape his head. My husband sniffs our son, lifts his arm by the wrist, rolls the joints to make sure everything arrived intact. "I think I should give him a bath."

"Okay," I tell him. "But remember to wrap his foot. You can use a ziplock bag and a rubber band, I think. I read that somewhere." Then I begin to unpack the CDs.

There is so much data to upload before he can enter fourth grade:

Motor Skills
English Language Recognition and Acquisition Software
Voice Recognition
Cognitive Behavior
Tone and Mood Modules

Obedience – Direct and Implied Commands
Hand-Eye Coordination
Automatic Reflexes
Levels 1-10 Conversation
Assertiveness and Confrontation (ON/OFF)
Automatic Response: Emergencies
Beginning Phonics
Beginning Spelling
Toilet Training
Handwriting (Male, Legible, D'nealian)
Levels 1-10 Music
Levels 1-10 Art
Levels 1-10 Speech and Pronunciation
Intermediate Phonics
Intermediate Spelling
Intuition Software
Sensitivity Module (Male, Average)
Auditory Processing
Deductive Reasoning
Beginning Numerics
Intermediate Numerics
Sensory Data Processing
Self-Sufficiency: Home Version: Levels 1-4
Self-Sufficiency: Public: Levels 1-4
Graphia/Calcula Recognition Software
Non-Verbal Learning
Visual Perception/Visual Motor Modules
Muscle Control and Coordination
Executive Functioning
Memory
Personality (Male, Average) (ON/OFF)
Level 1-10 Athletics
Level 1-10 Play (ON/OFF)

Interpersonal Relationships

Developmental Trust

...My eyes go blurry after a while.

We're not supposed to upload the CDs too quickly. They say that's how serial killers are made. We had a neighbor who tried to shortcut the process, uploaded their entire son in a week. We suspect they wanted him ready for their Viking river cruise in July. A few days after the upload my husband saw the boy plucking bird feathers from the bird bath next to the porch and sucking them like hard candy. Our neighbors left town shortly after that, and we haven't seen them since.

The manual makes it clear that we're meant to follow a specific schedule in uploading the CDs. There's even a color-coded calendar that we can unfold and stick to our fridge. Three months to build our son, complete by the 25th of August. But to see the CDs as a physical mass - 20 sons worth of data - makes the summer seem short, impregnable.

I can hear the bathwater running in the next room, the sound of a cup of warm water falling over my new son's head. It's amazing the tech they have now. Solar charging. Waterproof ports. Bluetooth capabilities. Voice Command software. But we couldn't afford all that. ALEX has the original tech, a port in his foot. His brain and nerves are mechanic, but the rest of him is organic. When I peer into the bathroom, my husband has ALEX's foot wrapped in plastic, balanced on the edge of the tub. We wanted a boy. A boy was what we could afford.

+

When I lay out all the CDs, they fill the entire dining table. They fill the side tables in our bedroom. They fill the living-room couch. A brilliance of color. Ten thousand terabytes. Tomorrow we'll plan and sort, but tonight, we put our new little boy into his brand-new bed.

His name is ALEX.

Username: ItsAlex847.

I remove the note pinned to his shirt. His bangs are still damp. I trim them with a pair of sewing scissors so they rest on his eyebrows. I can smell his breath through his nostrils – a sour, earthy smell. I kiss his forehead, even though I know he's sleeping. Sorry – in sleep mode. I keep forgetting: children are different these days. He won't grow up like my husband and I did. No one does.

So, I carefully screw the VGA cable into the port on the bottom of his foot, connect the other end of the cable to my laptop. I plug the laptop into a charger connected to this little standing bike I have. I spend a few minutes stretching before hopping on and starting to pedal. I've been doing this for a while now – generating enough for the washing machine cycles. Enough to microwave green beans. Enough to fill the backyard with light. Generating our own electricity has been a small way we've learned to save money. The manual says charging ALEX each night could add over $100 each month to our electric bill, and I'm grateful to have this alternative.

My husband and I take turns all night cycling, charging our new boy up.

+

In the morning, we're both exhausted, just like real new parents. But we've charged our laptop/son enough to access his data files. See through the little camera they have installed over his left eye. See the world he sees. His world.

We type "ItsAlex847" into the username portal and log-on to our new son. Well, he's our son after we complete the Welcome tutorial.

We hear the sound of a creaky door opening.

"Huh," my husband says. "Just like AOL."

We are expecting a large cache of files and photographs, perhaps the log-in credentials.

But it's a simple desktop. That bland green background from the 90's.

We double click the "LIVE Feed" icon (an almond eye) and it's black. In the corner of the desktop is a red and green switch we take to indicate power on and off.

"Do we turn him on?" I ask.

"Wait. Let's just," my husband says, and takes us through his paperwork. His electronic birth certificate and social, medical history, family history (all blank), receipt, and a brief letter:

Welcome! My name is ALEX, and I will be a great SON. If you have any questions or issues with your new SON, please call your Customer Service Representative. Have your serial number, username, and password ready.

I put my hand on the mouse, over my husband's hand. Together we click the power switch to green.

+

"Hello," I say to him.

ALEX sits up straight like he's been hit by lightning. His eyes are silver saucers. He tries to speak and finds he can't. He begins to cry. Silent sobs. Fat tears well in his eyes. He looks around the room and at his clothes and his hands, stands, winces at the cord connected to the port in his foot.

"Hey, it's okay, it's okay," I tell him, but my husband powers him down and ALEX slumps slowly to the floor, his eyelids falling shut.

My husband lifts ALEX back onto the bed, sets his head on the pillow. Then he himself slumps onto the floor and lies there with his hands over his eyes.

"Everything is scary the first time," I say.

"You're right."

"You would be disoriented, too."

"Uh huh."

I start to replay the LIVE feed, what ALEX saw when we turned him on, but my husband holds up a hand. I pause.

"We did the right thing, right?" he says. "We want this, right?"

"We did the right thing. We want this," I repeat.

My husband gets up, leaves the room. When I hear him in the kitchen, opening the fridge, running the faucet, I hit PLAY. I don't mind watching the video alone. This is a chance for me to form a special bond with our son. Share his first seconds of life, just like a real mother would.

The LIVE feed replay flickers on. I reach out and hold ALEX's ankle on the bed behind me. His skin is smooth and perfect.

The first thing our son saw was the ceiling and the rotating ceiling fan. When he sat up, the room was blurry around him. When he lifted his hand to his face, it was the only thing in focus. Everything else was splotches, like a watercolor before it dries. We haven't downloaded Shape Recognition yet. To ALEX, the world is a flat blur. The manual compares it to a blind person gaining sight for the first time. They can't reconcile the feeling of a *pear* to the image of a *pear*. The feeling of a loved one's face to the face itself. Still though, I can't help but feel a little disappointed.

I'd hoped ALEX would be able to push through the blur, to me.

+

The hardest part of parenting is prioritizing. Choosing what to learn first.

Some CDs we have to upload first. Our new ALEX can't sit up without teetering before we download BALANCE. So we give him BALANCE. ALEX needs Sight Software and Basic Motor Functions and Health and Wellness (Aversion to Poisons: ON, Diverse Food Interests: ON). He is heavy and doesn't know about facial expression yet. We have to carry him together those first days. I hold his head, my husband carries his legs. He pees on us because we haven't downloaded Toilet Training, and we can't download Toilet Training until the motor functions set in and he knows how to dilate his eyes and he learns to focus beyond the radius between his face and ours.

Other CDs, the manual says, we can upload to our own preference. For every day, there is a blank space on our color-coded calendar. Parents' Choice. We can't decide whether we want him to learn Musical Rhythm Recognition first or Concept of Zero. Do we want our son to be predisposed to be an artist or a mathematician? An architect or a motivational speaker?

My husband and I can't agree. I want to upload the Mathematical Reasoning package first. My husband thinks we should upload the optional CDs at random, blindly.

"Just like in the old days," he says. "A random soup of genetics. Our son should be allowed to discover what he's good at for himself, and us with him. Doesn't it feel a little—cold—to build him? Like he's a..."

He trails off. I wonder what kind of son we would have had if we did it the old way. Would he have my husband's red hair? Would his jaw crack every time he yawned like mine does? Would freckles scatter along his spine like they do on both of our backs?

But I didn't want a child the old way. I never wanted a baby. I never wanted to hold other people's babies. Whenever I imagined having a child, I imagined a boy or girl already grown.

"We'll take turns," I say. "I choose the CD today, and you can choose tomorrow."

I slip a CD on spatial reasoning into the laptop port, and our son's closed eyelids twitch.

+

It isn't long until the screaming starts. It takes new children weeks to apply the English Recognition Software – the manual calls this the "absorbing" phase. It's strange, seeing a boy scream like a baby, his lips trying to form syllables that turn into frustrated cries.

The manual encourages at least 8 hours of conversation a day to calibrate the dialect and vocabulary range of the family. This is hard to do while he screams, while his large body is behaving like an infant. Hard to do while he can barely chew and use a toilet. We try hard to speak in complete sentences around ALEX. We try to diversify our vocabulary. On the fridge, we have a list of alternate ways to say: this day is good, this day sucks, this day was fine. We don't want to inadvertently cast his language at the baseline: average, below-average.

My husband and I are surprised by how quickly we run out of things to say. To keep the conversation going, we start reading out loud to each other, while ALEX whimpers on the couch (even when it doesn't look like he is, the manual assures us, your BOY is listening). We read articles. *New Yorker* stories. *Washington Post* pieces. We try to find the most trustworthy news sources. We avoid publications that rely on logical fallacies to make their arguments. But one night I catch my husband reading ALEX *Goodnight Moon* before bed. I catch myself singing him the Irish lullaby my mother sung me. I daydream about our family, a few years from now, going on a vacation to the western coast of Ireland, kneeling on the grassy Cliffs of Moher while sea wind whips our hair, driving until we find my great-grandmother's gravestone and I can say to ALEX, *See—this is where you began.*

Though that would be a lie.

Sometimes I watch ALEX dream on the LIVE feed. All you see are clouds, moving across his retinas like a screensaver.

"You're going to be the smartest boy," I whisper as the clouds wisp by. "You are my best boy. My smart boy."

I still think of it as sleeping.

+

ALEX's first words are "tortoise migration."

We're sitting around the kitchen table, my husband helping ALEX to spoon couscous into his mouth, when ALEX gently pushes away the spoon and speaks.

It's so unexpected. My husband and I look at each other for a stunned second and then burst into laughter. We laugh until our eyes tear. It feels so good to laugh together that we forget for a moment to praise ALEX, to run to his side, to kiss his cheeks, to arrange our faces so that we make eye contact with him and he makes eye contact with us.

He's silent for the next few days after that, so we worry that it was a fluke, but then he whispers that the water is too hot during his morning bath. And the next day, as we watch a documentary about puffins, he comments that his favorite color is blue. Like this, he says, pointing to the glacier on the television screen. "No, honey," we tell him. "That is white. White like clouds. White like teeth." ALEX touches his lips. "White," he repeats. ALEX's voice is low and shy. As the days go by, he speaks more, and we learn that he says "caramel" like "car-mall," just like we do. And "pecan" like "pee-can," just like we do. Sometimes we think that he is just parroting us, but then he'll say something surprising, like, "Look! It's wild as green!" and I know this is real.

+

By July, ALEX can talk and walk by himself and use the toilet with 80% accuracy. I tell my husband that maybe it's time he goes back to work. He doesn't want to go, but I convince him that ALEX and I will be fine alone. I remind him that soon we'll be buying trapper keepers and ball point pens and new shoes for the first day of school. And later, entrance fees to the planetarium and soccer cleats and Christmas gifts wrapped in shiny paper. My job has given me paid parental leave, but my husband's has not. "Fine," he eventually says. "As long as you text me pictures. Pictures of everything. I mean it. If he's able to piss in the toilet without getting the floor wet, I want documentation."

The night before my husband goes back to work, I can't sleep. I'm giddy with anticipation. I hadn't realized how much I craved time by myself with ALEX. It makes me feel a little guilty how much I want it, like maybe I'm trying to push my husband out of the equation.

I wake up early, before my husband, to hop on the bicycle, to charge ALEX up to 100%. When he opens his eyes, he doesn't yawn or stretch. We didn't have the money for naturalisms like that. That's just something ALEX will need to learn via direct instruction. Right now, when ALEX wakes, he sits up straight to attention, knocking his plush tortoise to the floor. The tortoise we tried to get him to snuggle with, the tortoise we bought to commemorate his first words. Mostly it just gets knocked to the floor. We tried to get him to name it, but he didn't understand. "Hi, my name is ALEX," he said when we prompted him. "No, *name* the tortoise," we insisted. "My *name* is ALEX," he repeated. "That's my *name.*"

Little Alex lies shell down on the floor while big ALEX makes his bed. Part of his MORNING ROUTINE download.

"G'morning," he says, just like we do, making military corners. He peels off his pajamas and deposits them in the laundry basket. Pulls on clean underwear. Jean shorts. A blue and red striped shirt. Sensible sneakers. He marches off to the bathroom to wash up.

We need to work on his body language, I think. I wonder how much NONCHALANCE would cost, or some SOCIAL CUES modules. ALEX already has INTUITION but it doesn't seem to work in social situations. It mostly applies to food – detecting when something has spoiled. And sometimes he may say something odd, standing at his closet door. "I feel like red today," he might say. "I don't know why." And all day I'll catch him fingering the red sleeves of his shirt, smiling to himself.

He brushes each quadrant of his teeth for 45 seconds, gargles, spits. Some of it slides down the edges of the sink, and this makes me smile. I like seeing little cracks in the functionality. Makes it easier to believe he's real.

My husband stands in the doorway, tucking his shirttail

in, fussing with his beard. "You two going to be alright today?"

"Absolutely," I say.

He says, "Don't forget to download POP CULTURE. I don't want him being a weirdo in school."

"These CDs are from 2001. He'll be out of the loop by well over a decade."

My husband frowns. "2001 is better than nothing. It's cool to be into the classics." He hugs ALEX and kisses his forehead, right beside the camera lens protruding above the eyebrow, and heads out for the day.

ALEX puts his toothbrush back in its cup and stares at me, blinking once every 6 seconds. We listen to the hum of the garage door closing. ALEX's blinking is so steady I can measure time by it. 9 seconds for the garage door to shut. 15 seconds for the sound of my husband's car to fade as he drives away. Still ALEX doesn't move, and I realize he's waiting for instructions.

I don't know what to make of moments like this – is he just cooperating? Curious?

"We're going on a little trip," I say, taking his hand. I smile a conspiratorial smile. He tries to parrot it back to me, and I laugh. He laughs. In the 20 minutes it takes to download "POP CULTURE," I pack us a picnic, beach towels, sunscreen, plastic wrap, a small shovel and bucket. He sits on the edge of his bed watching me, kicking slightly with his plugged-in foot.

+

When we get to the beach, ALEX is immediately attuned to the sounds of waves. It's like I can see his ears bending forward like a horse's. His mouth gapes open as the salt air hits our skin. I breathe in deeply. "Welcome to the ocean, ALEX." I put a pair of small sunglasses over his eyes.

"Wow," he says, pressing them against his nose.

I say, "Isn't it neat?" I hoist the cooler and umbrella from the trunk and head toward the open beach. ALEX has a little trouble marching through the sand, his arms loaded down with towels, and I can't stop smiling. I love watching him like this.

He stares intently at the ocean tiding in and out. "Is it dangerous?" he asks.

"Not really," I tell him.

"What percentage of danger is it?"

I imagine shark fins, jellyfish, kelp tangles, waves cresting over his head. I imagine the unmapped bottom of the sea floor. Sunken ships and submarines. Underwater minefields. The tectonic plates shifting and spouting magma. What does ALEX already know about the ocean? "I'm not sure," I say.

We flap out our beach towels and sit on them pretzel style. We are almost the only people on the beach today. There is a man with a metal detector far enough away that his face is just a pink blob. I stick an umbrella into the sand and show ALEX how to crank it open. A circle of shade blooms around us. I help ALEX to ease off his shoes and socks and wrap the port-foot in plastic before slathering on the sunblock.

"This protects our skin," I explain, rubbing it into his neck and arms and across both cheekbones. "Do you know what a sunburn is?"

His eyelids flicker and then lock halfway over his eyes. He's thinking.

"Sunburn," he says, reciting. "Reddening, inflammation, and, in severe cases, blistering and peeling of the skin caused by overexposure to the ultraviolet rays of the sun."

"Uh, yes," I say. "Correct."

"Your skin can peel?" he asks, blinking at me.

I think of peeling apples, carrots, potatoes. What I say is, "Not if we protect it." I take ALEX's hand and lead him to the ocean. I say, "We are protected."

We stand at the edge of the tide. The waves rush in, foam at our feet, pool on ALEX's plastic wrap. It's cold. The hair on my body stands to attention. ALEX watches me wiggle my toes in the wet sand, then wiggles his.

I bend down, cup the waves in my hands, and splash the water over us.

ALEX wipes his eyes.

He looks up at me, squints against the sun. He says, "Drops of Jupiter in your hair."

I laugh. I take his hand. "It feels good, doesn't it?"

"It feels good," says ALEX. Affability: ON. Positive Affirmation: ON. "What is ultraviolet?" he asks.

"It has something to do with the sun," I say.

"You're not sure?" he says. Affability: ON. Critical Thinking: ON.

A wave covers our feet. It sprays our knees.

"It's okay to not be sure of something," I say. "Then we can have the fun of figuring it out."

A seagull coasts overhead, and ALEX's eyes go to it. I imagine him processing: black wing-tips, orange beak, fanned tail, webbed feet.

"ALEX," I say, and he turns to me like a kite tugged at its string. "When I look at the waves, I think of rolling fields of grass, like the ones we have behind our house. It makes me feel peaceful. What do you see when you look at the waves?"

His forehead crinkles. He looks out at the ocean.

"There's no wrong answer," I say.

"I see," ALEX answers slowly. "I see hills, too."

I should praise him for trying. I should say, "That's nice." I should say, "I guess we see the world the same way."

Instead, I take his hand—his fingers curl instinctively around mine—and walk him back to our towels.

+

When we return from the beach, I put ALEX into REST MODE, plug in the VGA cable and scroll through his Index. He does have some scientific and geographical knowledge of the ocean – I can find 'beach,' and 'sand,' and 'wave' – but when I click on 'wave' what comes up is

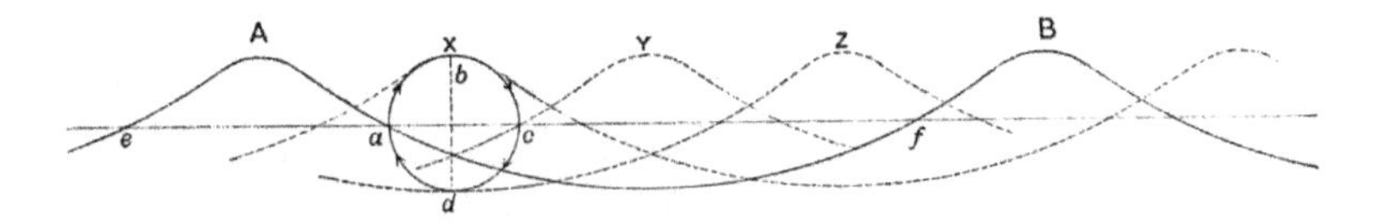

I wonder how to reconcile this data with our experience this morning. Where is the sting of the deep ocean water against our toes, the cleansing feeling of salty air on our cheeks? How was what happened this morning even filed? In the Index, I arrange by "Date Modified," and see this morning in a video file labeled FEED6-15-17. It's raw footage from his camera. ALEX didn't learn anything from me today.

In the Index, I click 'wave' again. There are executive editing functions, mostly for parental monitoring, and there's an additional information field I can type into.

I type:

I like the beach.

I type:

It feels good when the waves wash over my toes.

I type:

I wonder what's at the bottom of the sea.

Then I close the Index and close the computer. I lay next to ALEX in the bed. I put my nose in his hair and it smells like ocean. I feel for the heat of a sunburn on his forehead, but his skin is, as always, cool.

+

The next day, while my husband works, I take ALEX in for his first checkup. He needs to be up to date on vaccines and personally checked by a variety of doctors and technicians to ensure his functionality before the school year begins. We had this appointment scheduled before ALEX even arrived at our door.

"An older model, eh?" the pedia-tech says, winking at me. She's unscrewed a little plate in the back of ALEX's neck and is poking around the wiring in his neck, at the panel that acts as his brain. His foot is plugged into her computer and she has access to everything. His daily files. The curriculum we've downloaded. The stats that show how much lullabies affect his personality and mood.

"The new models are so over-priced," I say. Then, afraid I might have insulted her, add, "Not that it wouldn't be worth it."

I take out my camera phone and snap photos as she presses her fingers along ALEX's spine. My husband was upset that I'd forgotten to take pictures of ALEX at the beach—wouldn't talk to me all through dinner and insisted he put our son to bed by himself—and so I've decided to overdo it today. It's only 10 AM, and I've already sent 23 pictures.

As I text the newest photo to my husband, the tech says,

"I personally like the old models. More reliable. Predictable. Great parental oversight – you can see and access every data exchange. You've done a great job keeping this model up and running – he's in great shape."

I'm chewing my lips, wondering how many other children she sees like him. "Is he...is it obvious?" I ask. "Will the other children be able to tell?"

"Oh," she says, screwing the neck panel back in place. "You mean the full humans? Don't worry about that. So many kids are like ALEX these days. Let's see how the organics are doing."

She powers ALEX on.

She takes his temperature, checks his reflexes, blood pressure, weighs him (nearly 180 pounds, because of the mechanical aspects), peers in his ears and nose and mouth. She asks, "How are you doing ALEX?" and he says, "Not too shabby." Just like us.

She taps his knee with a reflex hammer and ALEX says, "I wonder what's at the bottom of the ocean."

The pedia-tech looks from him to me, puzzled.

"We went to the beach yesterday," I explain.

"I like the beach," says ALEX, a small buzzing coming from inside of his head. He scratches at it. "The sun looked like a lightbubble."

"Huh," says the tech. "Spontaneous thought. I didn't know the old modules had those configurations. What year did you say he was?"

"2006."

"Nice. My Toyota's an '06." She sticks a flashlight into his ear. "Well, it isn't overheating him. That can happen sometimes. You may want to install a fan across his neck panel if you ever notice it, though."

I thank her, take ALEX by the hand. When we leave, I see

a waiting room full of children I can't tell are humanoid or not. The point is to not be able to tell. There's a skinny man in a suit, a baby small as a flour sack balanced against his chest while he checks his phone. The baby isn't crying.

Rest mode, I instinctively think.

"Why do 'I wonder'?" ALEX asks.

"You wonder why you wonder?" I say mysteriously.

There's a whirring coming from his ear. It feels loud, like the whole room can hear it.

+

Every day while my husband is at work, I update something in ALEX's Index.

I discover connotation preferences. Dialect choices. Associations. I can actually hear the digital synapses (they make a sort of clicking) inside ALEX's head when I fuss with them on the laptop. Sometimes he stays in sleep mode all afternoon so I can update the Index with memories.

Well, I think of them as memories. I prefer 'memories' to 'indexes.'

Under 'soft' I update associations: kittens, clouds, white beach sands, skin, cotton quilts, the look of snow.

Under 'Wednesday' I make sure the pronunciation is 'WED-NESS-DAY" (internally), just like me.

Under worries, I start inserting my own:

I worry I won't fit in.

I worry I stomp my feet when I walk.

I worry that my face looks weird when I'm thinking.

I worry my references will be out of touch.

I upload pictures of my childhood home, the mosquito-riddled lake, the hills covered in snow, the kitchen with the yellow tiles and large windows, and set them on his daydream rotation.

Under 'sexuality,' I hesitate. There is a censorship option here, to nix any content containing language from a black list. I'm not sure how I feel about this, the list of body parts and gendered slang. I erase 'ejaculation,' 'hard-on,' 'climax' from the blacklist. I write something about consent and love and the importance of male birth control in the additional notes box. I write, Masturbation isn't bad.

I upload my favorite songs to be stuck in his head.

I tease out preferences for toothpaste, ice-cream, chewing gum flavor.

I tamper with the sensitivity module. Turn it to MAX.

II.

It's been six months since we downloaded Stage Four Puberty.

And it's been five years since ALEX became our son.

ALEX has been avoiding me for days.

On Friday he locked the door to his bedroom and refused to come to dinner. It's been hard because he needs me to power him up, so he sticks the cord underneath his door, and I bike and bike until he's had enough and gives a yank, the cord snaking back under the threshold.

My husband thinks it's gross and invasive that I've been monitoring ALEX's masturbation habits, so I stop telling him when I check. I stopped telling my husband everything a long time ago, so it's not hard to hide one more thing.

I don't tell my husband that I think it's sweet how chaste ALEX's fantasies are. In the video replays, it's all pink softness behind his eyelids. It's bare shoulders and jawlines and smooth kneecaps. I have an app on my phone now. I can check ALEX's logistics as I wait in traffic.

When ALEX finally leaves his room, he says, "Mom, I'm so sick of you invading my privacy. I know you've been in my head."

I'm in the living room drinking a ginger ale and watching a reality TV show about a humanoid searching for love. The girls don't know he's a humanoid, and the humanoid worries that they will break up with him when they find out. I change the channel to a golf game as ALEX enters the room, because I don't want him thinking being a humanoid makes him any different from other people.

"Mom," he says, standing in front of the television, "I feel like my thoughts are really your thoughts."

This is the first time ALEX has let on that he knows what I do inside his head while he's sleeping.

I take a breath. I say, "Honey, that's just what it means to be someone's offspring. Every child is a composite of the genetics their parents pass on to them and the ideas their parents' expose them to."

I think to how I downloaded Phobias and Neuroses and Panic Attacks when ALEX was twelve to help him seem more natural. How I turned Affability: OFF. How I gave him my Fear of Heights and watched him panic when we rode a ski-lift to the top of an alpine slope and how he was so terrified that when we got to the bottom again he ran into the bathroom and refused to come out.

"No," ALEX says. "What I mean is, last week I had the thought that the neighbors were judging me because the paint on the mailbox was chipping. Why would I think that? I don't even know the neighbors' names. Mom? And why can't I drink Pepsi anymore? Why does it feel like slugs crawling down my throat when I drink it?"

"You were drinking too much soda," I say. "It was making you break out."

ALEX throws his hands outward and lets out a frustrated groan that he must have picked up at school. He stomps out of the room, and I hear his bedroom door slam.

When I hear his lock click, I tiptoe upstairs and put my ear to the door. I hear tinny music and tapping and know he must be playing one of his video games. ALEX can hold his pee for three times as long as a normal teenager. He won't be out anytime soon. I sink to the ground and lean my back to ALEX's door and try to get comfortable.

+

After my maternity leave ended, I didn't go back to work like I'd said I would. My husband got a second job transcribing phone calls for the hard of hearing so we could afford to pay for the first stage of Puberty CDs, and suddenly the most time we ever spent together was in the morning, bumping into each other between the fridge and Keurig.

At the end of the first summer I brought up the idea of homeschooling ALEX, but my husband convinced me that the best way for him to learn to be a real boy (we've learned to stop using words like "real" since then) was to be around kids his biological age. So instead, I spent my days reading books on parenting. I learned how to sew. I learned how to cut the crust off sandwiches while preserving the maximum amount of bread. I learned how to turn cardboard boxes and white sheets into costumes for the school play.

And ALEX became a dream son. He became the person I wish I'd been when I was a child. On his report cards, teachers wrote that he was a real upstander. That he cried when pigeons got stuck in the gymnasium after recess. He always asked his peers for their preferred pronouns.

I told him how proud I am of him, but he never

understood pride. He was acting the only way he knew how.

+

As I wait outside ALEX's door, I worry. I worry about ALEX in a way I've never had to worry about him before. I worry that he will hate me or already does. I worry about him becoming a son who closes his laptop when I come into the room. I worry about him downloading malicious software that could negatively augment his bloodstream or overheat him. I worry about him sneaking off somewhere with low cell-reception because, I realize, ALEX is one giant mobile computer. I worry about him powering down suddenly on a hike, or getting waterlogged and having his electronic synapses electrocuting his organic parts. He knows he's not allowed to swim, sunbathe, rock-climb, hike. I picture broken bones and computer chips. Sometimes on the weekends I power him to nearly off and run diagnostic after diagnostic. I check the ALEX app probably 60 times a day, that little blinking GPS dot that tells me where he is, his mainframe temperature, his heartrate.

Is this what it feels like to be the mother of a biological child, a child whose brain is separated from you by six millimeters of hard skull?

I hear ALEX sleeping. ALEX puts himself on SLEEPMODE now. It's a privilege we gave him after he turned thirteen. I wait a minute just to be sure, and then I get a hair pin from the bathroom and pick the lock and open the door slowly so it won't squeak. Not that a squeak would wake him, but there are still things that are different about him that I forget.

I want to log into ALEX's main frame. I want to hunt down what went wrong like a dog hunting down a fox. The ALEX app's functions are limited, and I haven't been able to figure out if defiance and heightened self-awareness are a normal part of the Stage 4 Puberty Program.

My son is belly-down on his twin bed, arms outstretched and hanging over the edges. His mouth is open, and I can feel the softness of face, of his vulnerability, without even having to touch him.

I sit down at the swiveling desk chair and turn the computer on. I place my thumb on the password key, but nothing happens. I type in the backup password, and again nothing. I check if I accidentally hit CapsLock. An error message comes up and tells me that I have exceeded the maximum number of password attempts. Another failed attempt will result in a temporary shut-down of the subject.

There's a knock on the door frame. It's my husband. He's still in his work clothes, pressed khakis and striped button-up, badge clipped to his pocket.

"Something malfunctioned when I tried to upload his English Class essay on domestic violence," I say.

He enters the room, sits on the mattress next to ALEX. ALEX's body lifts and then settles. I can't see his expression when he says, "Liar."

I pretend I didn't hear what my husband said.

I try booting the computer down and repowering it back on. This trick used to work all the time when ALEX froze or he got a bug.

But when I log back in, there's a new username portal. One for ItsAlex847. One for Guest.

When I log in as Guest, there is just an empty desktop with the background text GET OUT OF MY HEAD.

I look to my husband.

"You heard him," he says.

"Do you think he's okay? Maybe we should wake him?"

"How would we do that?"

I spider my fingers down the cord that connects our son to the machine and let them rest on his ankle. There are wiry hairs where his foot turns into leg. I twist them between my thumb and forefinger. They feel real.

My husband doesn't leave the room and neither do I. I join him on the bed.

My husband unclips his badge, slides his shoes off, says, "It's funny. I don't see myself in him."

But he doesn't know the parts of him I slipped into ALEX's personality. Things I remember liking in my husband when we first met, before I had any idea we'd marry, before I really knew him at all. The way he was always grammatically correct in text messages – he'd even use semicolons. How at parties he always slipped beer bottlecaps into his back pocket, even ones that didn't belong to him. How he'd talk to every dog he met on the street. I'd seen ALEX do that too, bending down towards the neighbor's Yorkshire and tasseling her ears. Saying, "Howdy," like we do, when we're goofy.

I must have fallen asleep with my hand on ALEX's ankle, because next thing I know the room is full of yellow light. Birdsong through the open window. Low clouds. Wet that clings to the bedsheets, the carpets, like the porch after a thunderstorm.

My husband is awake and watching me. His hair sticks up in the back.

ALEX is sleeping.

I look at my watch.

ALEX should be awake by now, but still ALEX is sleeping.

"We should dress him," my husband says.

I nod, and we work together to lift his limp, fleshy torso, to pull off his white, cotton undershirt, to pull on his school polo, pull it over and around the angles of his elbows, his shoulders.

My husband lifts our son's legs, one at a time, so I can tug jeans up over his hips. Then, we each put a hand under an armpit and lift ALEX into the sitting position.

"Looking good, ALEX," my husband says. "Now it's time to wake up, or you're going to be late for Calculus. We know how much you love Calculus."

ALEX's head lulls against his chest.

"Oh, I don't know," I say. "ALEX works so hard, maybe we should just let him take a day off."

"Maybe we should all take a day off," my husband says.

We slump on the floor beside the bed, beside ALEX, over the covers, and lean our heads against each others. I can feel my husband's warmth against my cheek. We haven't slept like this in ages. ALEX rolls over and his hand lolls off the bed. I take it. I burrow my nose against his skin and breathe in. And realize, he smells just like us.

III.

There is this fear I have of ALEX spontaneously shutting down. For the past few years there have been reports of humanoid sons and daughters on the fritz. Overheating errors. A drive that completely wipes itself. The constant whirring when a humanoid has maxed out his memory capacity. We've been trying to help ALEX by purchasing him a series of external drives for Calculus, for Physics and AP Lit and Honors Latin, that he can connect via USB during class. But in a couple of years we'll have to make the choice whether or not or wipe him. Or, really, what to wipe. ALEX doesn't have the capacity for childhood memories and college, for BALANCE and this new relationship he's started with Heather, a biological from his Latin class. He doesn't have room for Aerospace Engineering and Poetry and the Old Navy Employee Handbook and wondering what lies at the bottom of the ocean. I'll have to take away almost everything I gave him in those early days. Take back what he no longer seems to want.

Thing is, I can't access it as Guest.

I hate that word, Guest.

I consider hiring a hacker I find online. He quotes me ten thousand to re-personalize my son. Two thousand to wipe.

I erase my browser history.

I put my laptop into a drawer with a lock.

Pull out my phone since I can't resist the internet.

I read humanoid horror stories on Facebook.

HELP! MY DAUGHTER RESTARTED AND I LOST **EVERYTHING!**

'DAVID' WAS DATAMINED. THEN MY WHOLE FAMILY WAS.

I BETATESTED FOUR NEW SONS AND NOT ONE COULD SURVIVE THIS SIMPLE MALWARE TEST.

MY DAUGHTER'S BATTERY WARPED. WHAT HAPPENED NEXT WILL SHOCK YOU.

I curl into the oversized easy-chair in the den, the darkest, snuggest place in the house. I tap out an email to ALEX, apologizing for putting thoughts into his head. Tell him if he's ready to have 'the talk,' we can discuss erasure options.

I sign off "Respectfully, Mom."

A few hours later, I mute the television. From upstairs, I hear the creak of a bed.

+

ALEX and I go on a vacation to the western coast of

Ireland.

We leave without telling my husband.

He thinks we're going to school but really ALEX and I are getting on an airplane. Taking a suitcase I packed and hid surreptitiously in the trunk of my car.

I decide to give ALEX space on the flight over. I've told him this whole experience is about space – about finding your roots and running away from them at the same time. I imagine I can hear the music coming from inside ALEX's ear but do my best not to lean on him, not even when I fall asleep, instead resting my head against the window.

ALEX wakes me up before the plane lands.

"Mom," he says. "I've been thinking a lot and I know what I want."

My phone pings. I open an email from ALEX and it's a picture of an old typewriter.

"You want to go offline?"

He looks at me without blinking. "No more CDs, no more Apps. I want to be the only one inside my head."

"I won't be able to help you anymore," I say. "I won't know if you need help."

He takes a breath. "I won't erase anything without transcribing it first," he says. "But I want you to know I'm going to keep some things. I'm going to keep the stuff about the ocean."

He squeezes my hand like he's the parent. He says, "I'm going to keep being mad at you."

I look at him. I listen to the buzzing and snapping sounds his mechanical parts make.

"Okay," I say.

We sit in silence a long time. He's still squeezing my hand, and I'm trying to imprint that sensation into a permanent place in my body. I'm trying to imprint what it feels like, him looking at me deeply like this.

He says, "I'm going to keep what I love about you."

I say, "Me too. What I love about you. You."

When we land in Ireland, we take a cab to the cliffs. The wind is cold and wild. We lay our suitcase behind a rock. We break the rules about climbing and scale the rocks in our bare feet. We drink warm cups of soup and talk about what lies at the bottom of the sea.

I ask him what he really believes. What he wonders about.

This time, I listen.

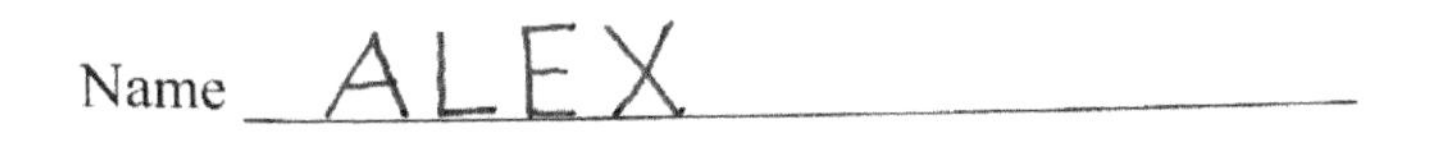

Describe this image from 2 or more perspectives. For example, how might it feel from the man's perspective, or the perspective of the man, or from the viewer (the man who watches), the man's father or son, or a man somewhere isolated (as in space).

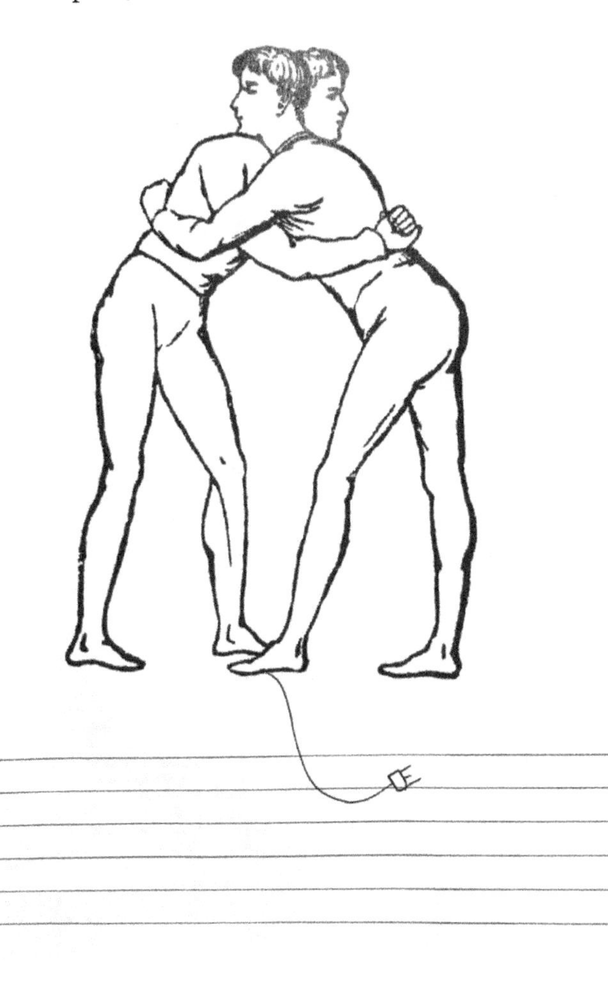

THE CLASSROOM BENEATH OUR CLASSROOM

Sometimes in the gaps between lessons, those rare moments when no one is whispering or coughing or tapping their marker against the desk legs or humming without knowing it or sharpening their pencil, we hear them. The classroom beneath our classroom.

The classroom beneath our classroom is better behaved than we are. We hear them reciting their times tables in unison, no voice hollering above the rest, no voice speaking a beat out of sync. In the morning they say the Pledge, and they sound like they mean it—not mean, half sarcastic, like we do.

+

Our classroom is on the ground floor, so there shouldn't be a classroom beneath our classroom, and yet there is. The students' voices rise up through the pipes, through the vents. Sometimes—when we're doing jumping jacks to test our heart rate, or when the teacher's back is turned and we're testing our limits, seeing how loud we can get before she quiets us, when we all holler "here" when the teacher calls Marcy's name even though she's been absent all week—we hear a rapping against the floor, a quick staccato, and we all freeze, imagining the wood of a ruler *slap slap slapping*. Sometimes instead of a slapping it's a thump, a broomstick sound, or the *whack* of the students all closing their books together, loudly.

When it happens, we look down.

I can hear you, it says, that slam below us. *I know exactly what you're up to.*

Sometimes we think it's all in our heads, this classroom beneath our classroom. And sometimes we hear our teacher mumbling, in a way she thinks we can't hear. Her back turned, scribbling on the board, she mutters, "I ought to send you to *her* classroom. Then you'll really miss me. Then you'll realize how easy you have it."

We ask if she's ever met the teacher in the classroom beneath our classroom, and she tells us to put our feet on the floor, that there's only two minutes of class yet, that we've lost recess time.

If one of us is misbehaving she'll say, "I'm this close to asking you to leave my classroom. If you can't handle being a fourth grader today..." And her gaze arrows down, and we know we're not just imagining things.

Sometimes we feel guilty for being the class that we are. The class that invokes exasperated looks between teachers in the hallways. The class that gets the field trip to the county jail instead of the zoo. The class that teachers swear prompted Mrs. Philips to have a stroke when she had us in second grade.

But other times we love to be that class. Love to be the class that started a petition to stop Miss Thomas from wearing purple eye shadow on Mondays. The class that had a water bottle of vodka hidden under the slide on the playground for a whole month before one of the monitors discovered it. Love to be the class that spits, that hollers, that isn't afraid when a teacher says they're disappointed in us. Love watching that split, like watching a seam come loose, when a teacher gives up on us, gives in, just lets us jump chair to chair or punch each other in the throat, who resigns herself to her desk, behind her computer, rubbing her temples, where she belongs.

+

On the playground, we try to identify the kids from the classroom beneath the classroom. We expect them to be paler than us, part mole creature. We expect them to have inhalers in their pockets and pencil pouches containing only sharpened pencils. We expect them to have hair parted down the middle and T-shirts with the tags carefully clipped off so they're never in danger of popping out.

We imagine being locked away with teachers underground so long kind of turns you into one.

We find kids who we think fit the description. But they are all friends of our siblings, or neighbors, or kids we know from a different year. No one's heard of the students who learn beneath.

We think about how we've seen the staircase that goes upstairs, but never the staircase that goes downstairs. One day we get curious and look for the downstairs staircase that must exist somewhere between our classroom and the front office. We feel the floors with our hands for a loose tile, a trapdoor. We stage a food-fight and get the boys in our grade to pee all over the toilet paper in the restroom while an elite team crawls on their bellies toward the teachers' lounge, hunting for clues. We tap the walls, listen for a hollow sound. Maybe it's behind a locker. Maybe it starts on the roof, that one locked door only the buff PE teacher has a key to. We're convinced we're hearing things. Our ears prick up when we hear footsteps.

One day the classroom below us is learning jiu jitsu, and

we hear the technique, the lessons, and...it's the voice of a child. A young girl, about our age. It's a quiet voice, it's hard to hear through to one floor when our teacher is trying to get us to understand figurative language, so we have to get quiet. We fold our hands. Our ears stretch around the sound of whiteboard markers. I drop a pencil so I can crawl under my desk to better pick up the sound.

The voice below us says, "A smaller, weaker person can successfully defend against a bigger, stronger assailant by using proper technique, leverage, and most notably, taking the fight to the ground." I can't tell if she is reading from a book or reciting. She sounds strong. I hear a tap against a whiteboard and the scribbling of notes, 30 pencils simultaneously. "In side control, you pin your opponent to the ground from the side of his body." Where did she learn to talk like this? I hear a smart set of footsteps descending what sounds like the south wall of our classroom, and the classroom below us stirs. The girl's voice stops. A door opens and closes. "I'm so impressed," says the teacher in the classroom beneath our classroom. "You're the only class in school who behaves even when I step out. Maybe we'll even get recess tonight. I'll make a special call to the night crew."

I freeze under my desk my pencil in hand. My teacher taps on my desk, says, "Back in your seat," and I do it, mummified.

+

All week we've been behaving. Our teacher seems pleased, pats us on the heads, says, "You've really grown," says, "I'm writing a note to your parents about this new positive attitude." But really we've just been listening. Waiting for the switch that happens when the teacher in the classroom below our classroom steps out, how the students seem to turn towards one voice, a girl who seems to stand on her chair, and says, "We have only this choice. No one is coming for us." She sounds older, her voice deep, serious.

Our hearts strain in our sweatshirts. It's winter. We wonder how cold it is to stay underground. We wonder if they live there. They must, since we've never seen them. The classroom below our classroom is learning how to knit, how to quilt. They ask sharp, inquisitive questions during class. When the teacher steps out, we hear someone reading from (what we presume is contraband) survival books, books on escape. Now that we've started listening, we can hear so much that we couldn't hear before.

At recess, we convene under the double slide, mittened hands cupping mouths, knees touching.

"We should tell someone," one of us says. "We should see the principal. Demand answers. Those kids are being held against their will."

"No, no," the rest of us say. "All of the adults are in on this. We can't let them know what we know."

The girl's voice had awakened something in us. A desire to turn all of our spitting and lying and fighting into something of storybooks, something of heroes. When the playground monitor walks by us, we lean in closer, digging our knees into the woodchips.

We create a Plan.

It's decided that since I live closest to the school, since I have a ground floor window, since I bike to school, anyway, it makes the most sense that I'm the one to carry out the Plan. I will do it during a full moon so I don't get caught with my flashlight. They will choose the night for me, on my behalf. It is starting to feel like my class is one entity and I am another one, separate, just me.

+

I think about writing a letter before I go. I start one—*Dear Mom, Dear Dad, Dear Classmates*—but throw it out before I get any farther. Writing a letter feels too much like giving up. I slip out my window in a thick sweater, my mother's cellphone in my back pocket, a windup flashlight for once I get to the school. I have our teacher's security pass, which we swiped when we "accidentally" knocked over all the graded work on her desk, and when we went in a mad rush to "help" her. You'd be amazed what teachers don't notice when we encircle them like a swarm. It isn't even that hard.

Outside the grass is frosted and the moonlight hits the hoods of cars, the eyes of cats, the glass windows of the school building. I think about how easy it would be to go back home now, to tell my classmates that I hadn't found anything and leave it there. But then I remember the girl and her voice. The girl who'd given up on rescue but would be so grateful once it came.

The security key works. I'd half wished it wouldn't. The whole school is dark and my shoes are so loud on the concrete floors I echo. I slip them off. I want to come in stealth. I want to not be known. I have no idea where the staircase is, so I start by going to my classroom. What I know for certain is they're below me, and if they're in there all the time, this is my best bet. I go into the classroom and lay my ear against the tile. I don't hear anything. I mean, I hear the humming of a street lamp outside, I hear my heart coming up for air. The fluids in my ears are making noises. I knock against the ground with one knuckle. Then I think I hear someone cough.

"Hello? Is someone down there?"

I hear a rustling, but that could be anything, could be me hearing my hearing, repositioning my body so my ear is against the floor.

"I hear you all the time," I say, loud enough to be heard below. "I want to meet you. I want to help you."

But it's quiet. Maybe they're all sleeping. Maybe they go somewhere else to sleep.

"If you can hear me, do something. Tap the top of your classroom with a broomstick. Close a book. Cough again."

And while I'm waiting for something to happen, my classroom doors open. And there's a flashlight beam so bright I can't see who's holding it. The flashlight, I mean. I mean, the beam is beaming into my eyeballs, and I can't see, but they seem tall. They're strong when they grab me. "Hey," I shout. "Don't touch me. Let go of me," and I rip myself away, run through the door, am moving backwards, sideways. I can't see because of the beam that blew up my eyeballs, and next thing I know I'm stumbling down the stairs. How can I be stumbling down the stairs, how could they have been here all along? And when I hit the last step, I know it. I'm where the other ones are. I'm beneath the real school.

+

It's hard to tell how much time is passing down here. We don't have clocks. We can't see the sun. It could be 4 in the morning and we're learning algebra. I don't know algebra yet. Down here, I'm the stupid one, I'm exotic, my skin is so brown.

I keep my eyes peeled for the girl, I keep waiting for her to raise her hand so I can know her by her voice. Maybe this isn't her room. Maybe there is a classroom beneath every classroom, and I've stumbled into the wrong one. When the teacher leaves us to get some coffee – maybe to see some sky? – we don't get out of our seats. Some of the kids close their eyes. Some of them scratch their knees. I lean over to one, recognize her. Marcy. We all just thought she got sick or switched schools. She looks so different down here. A shadow version of herself. I say, "Marcy, let's see what's in her desk. I can guard the door." But she turns me in when Ms. Maypole returns. Ms. Maypole is skinny and smile-less. She stands behind me when I say the Pledge. I am learning the meaning of fervor, and not just because I am memorizing the dictionary one letter at a time.

While Ms. Maypole is passing out worksheets, I ask my elbow-partner who the girl is who knows jiu jitsu.

Ms. Maypole doesn't have to turn around. "Someone doesn't want recess tonight," she says, and that gives me hope. Night recess means outside, means above-ground, means a chance.

I start to form new plans. The playground is surrounded by a concrete wall that no kid has ever been able to climb. I brainstorm on the corner of my paper, pretending to calculate the degrees of angles. I could toss a note wrapped around a rock. I imagine my old classmates waiting on the other side with open palms. Classmates who've been forming their own plans, who haven't stopped strategizing under the slide at recess. Maybe they've left a message for me there, maybe they're tunneling under the walls now, chipping away at tree roots and concrete, passaging my way out.

I behave through trigonometry and phonics and Latin—feet on the floor, eyes on the board, I pretend to be a good kid. When it's time for history, the teacher separates us into small groups. It's the first time I've left my seat since I arrived. In this classroom beneath the classroom, erasers never seem to wear away, pencils are always sharp. I can't sense the passage of time. Maybe we exist outside of it. My legs tingle as I stand.

In our small groups, we're told to prepare presentations on the make-up of a plant cell. As the others shuffle around the desks, a boy I've never noticed—a boy with blonde, side-combed hair and dark-rimmed glasses and thin wrists—sidles up to me. He murmurs to me without turning his head, "She's not here anymore."

"Who?" I ask, though I know he means the girl.

When he speaks, his lips barely moved. "She wanted to get us out. She wanted us to fight, but they caught on. They always do."

"Where did they take her?"

He says that he didn't notice her leave. At some point, he just realized she was gone.

I notice for the first time that there are the perfect number of students for desks in the room. There was a desk ready for me when I arrived. How long was this desk empty before it was mine?

"Maybe she found a way out," I said. "Maybe at recess."

He looks at me for the first time. He looks at me strangely.

And I understand, there is no recess.

When I return to my desk, I search its surface for messages written in eraser that you can only see from an angle, for scratched initials. But the desk's surface is impossibly smooth. I don't even find my own fingerprints.

+

The weird thing is, the thing I can't get over, is that I can't hear them. The classroom above our classroom. I realize now that the thumps we heard from time to time, coming from beneath the floor, had nothing to do with us. I wonder if my old classmates are listening for me. I wonder if somewhere they have their ears pressed to tile, waiting for my voice to rise above the rest. I wonder if I'm in a room that no one else is above.

School Blueprint

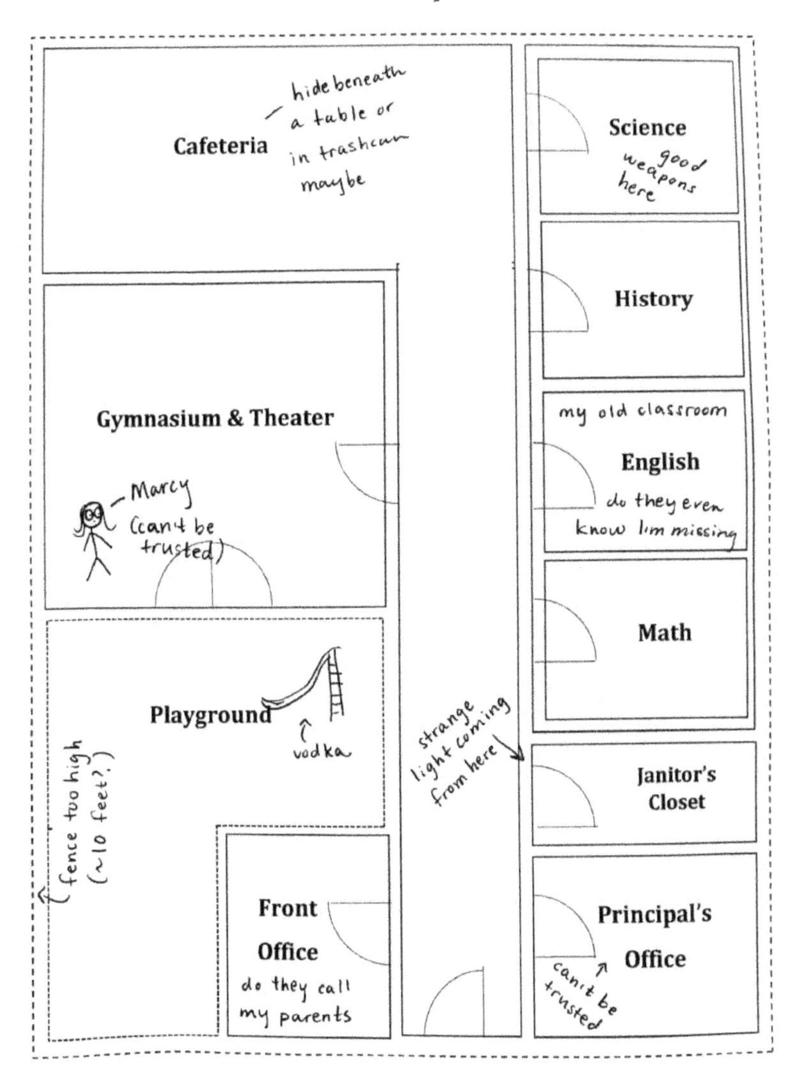

THE 41ST BEE

I don't know what to do with the bees. I don't know whether to treat them as forty-one individuals or one collective. They show up in third week of spring, an hour into second period. I clear a space next to one of my first graders, and awkwardly pull out the chair. The bees land on the seat, the top of the desk, the desk edge. One bee lands on my hand that I've used to gesture. I ask the boy sitting beside the bees to point to the words in the book we've been reading, so the bees can follow along. I can't tell if the bees are paying attention. They're humming, their little wings making a zip-unzip sound. I get nervous when I turn back to the chalkboard.

At the end of class, the bees don't know they are dismissed. They linger at their table. They think it's theirs now. I say, "Time to go to science," and try to cup them in my hands. I am worried that they'll sting me, but they do not. They spill out from my hands like water. They fly up to the ceiling. They buzz against the chalkboard. They slip into the crooks of my desk.

When I was a younger teacher, I might have held each bee in my hand, found its gaze, placed each in a glass jar with a single candy, written a note about how each ~~person~~ bee makes a difference.

I would have stayed late making sure my penmanship was just right.

I would have worn an ironed dress the next day, worked

my hair into a bun big as a hive.

Instead I turn the AC down to very, very cold, so the bees' instincts kick in and they migrate to the hallway.

+

Usually we pin notes to students when we have important documentation to send home, but you can't pin notes to bees. In the parking lot after school, I walk with them. I carry a permission slip in my hand. I am wondering if the museum will even admit them, or the bus driver – but I can't worry about that now, escorting a swarm across a parking lot. The bees land on my earlobe. They land on the hem of my skirt, my bangs. I can feel them through my leggings and dress-shirt and shoes. "This is my personal space," I say when we've arrived to the parent pick-up space. "Please don't land on my cheek without permission." Meanwhile I am looking for their mother. *Some queen bee?* I'm thinking. I glance at the insides of flowers, at the leaves of trees. I feel like my skin is unzipping itself.

But it is a stout woman who arrives, wearing beekeeping gear and high-tops. She opens a large black purse and the bees all fly in.

"I hope they behaved themselves today," she says, taking the permission slip and turning away in one movement, without even waiting for an answer.

+

It's very hard for the bees during exams. They never stay behind their privacy folder, and their table partners complain that the bees are cheating. It's very hard for the bees to free read. As a collective, they struggle to lift a pencil, to turn a page, to return a dictionary to a shelf. A teacher-friend shows me how to make copies at a twelfth the regular size. She suggests I trim out tiny worksheets, staple them together into bee-sized booklets. But I know the other children would be jealous. They don't understand that fairness sometimes means different treatment. That some of us have the advantage of a brain big as a baseball. That some of us have the privilege of operating not as a collective, but as one.

+

It is difficult to find something that retains the interest of all 41 bees at once. I decide to do a unit on space. A rocket is being launched in two weeks, a rocket that will carry astronauts to the moon. The launch pad is close enough to the school for us to see the cottony trail of smoke from our classroom window. I thought the bees would like this, learning about the rotation of planets, the mechanics that propel a body of hollow metal into the sky. But they are only interested in their own flight. As I lecture on the difference between a solar and lunar eclipse, they hover over orange peels in the trash. They crawl around inside the classroom pencil sharpener.

"You need to make accommodations for them," our ELL Instructor tells me. "You're speaking too fast. You need to act out the words of the story for the bees to understand."

I try to look at her like I'm not imagining her as a punctured balloon.

I try to take a breath before I return to class, but even now I can hear the hum of them. That tiny lawnmower-ing sound they make as they find their chair. I spend a minute of class trying to locate who is murmuring before a student in the front row points behind her and mouths, “It’s them. It’s the bees.”

Even when I am acting out the hoot of an owl or the way one character falls into a lake, I can’t tell if the bees understand. I’m not sure if the bees should be penalized when one bee lands on a student’s desk and breaks its stinger off on a notebook. I’m not sure what to do with the four or five bees who’ve left their desk and are batting their bodies against the window on the south-facing wall. “Bees, please sit down,” I say, embarrassed that I haven’t learned their names. The following day I receive a curt email from the woman who takes them home, and she has made a list of their names and writes “I encourage you to learn them”:

1. Tracy
2. Eveline
3. Angel
4. Mikayla
5. Micky
6. Mike
7. Misty
8. Mindy
9. Merryl
10. Mayson
11. Maddie
12. Mendel
13. May
14. Tony
15. Torrence
16. Ty
17. Tina
18. Tiny
19. Clarence

20. Clarice
21. Kristen
22. Katherine
23. Catherine with a C
24. Katie
25. Kaylie
26. Kylie
27. Kieley
28. Kiera
29. Kate
30. Katarina
31. Katrina
32. Kayce
33. Kurt
34. Lisa
35. Leeroy
36. Rome
37. Yulia
38. Ulysses
39. Erin
40. Aaron with an A
41. Air

+

After school I spend hours with the bees trying to help their swarm function as hands. I get them to write the letter A. I try to use some of their names. I try not to bat the air. I hope the other teachers notice the extra effort I'm putting in. I swat a wasp with my lesson plan and worry that the bees will see it as a betrayal. They're probably always being mistaken for wasps. I try to ignore it when one of the bees lands on my nose, and crawls in circles there. I try not to picture the couch in my sister's apartment I've been sleeping on, or the line of ants I've seen zig-zagging outside her door, or the squeaky sound of her tennis shoes when she gets up early to go for a run. I try to tell the migraine in my mind "Hello," as my therapist suggested, try imagining the migraine taking a seat beside me at the table full of bees, try imagining the migraine as company and not a permanent fixture clipped to my forehead.

I go back to the alphabet. I tell the swarm the second letter is theirs, and they fizz and fuzz and contort until they master it: B B B.

+

I don't know what to do with the bees. They still can't write their names. My boss comes to my room on Monday morning before the students arrive and asks, "Do you know what this is about?" He tells me. The bees' keeper sent him an email lamenting that the bees felt they were being ignored. They weren't making friends. They'd started acting out at home. This was not what they had been promised from our school.

The next day I leave wildflowers on the bees' desk. I dab my fingernails with honey enzymes. I open the windows so the sweet smell of cut grass fills the room, but that triggers all of the other students' allergies. I make 41 name-tags for their desk, and print each of their names in efficient teacher cursive. But the bees do what bees do.

On the playground, they swarm into hand-formation and flip a beetle on its back. They crowd-surf on some kid's dropped sandwich. A handful of bees returns to class late with cheese-dust on their wings, and one of my students is crying and accusing them of eating his Doritos, though of course he can't know for sure if it was our bees or a wild bee out on the playground. Every day, I hear a new complaint:

"A bee poked me in the hallway."

"I think I was stung during music class."

"They won't get out of my lunchbox."

"They keep flying across my eyes."

We watch a video on bullying, and when the lights come back on, half of the class raises their hands. "I think we're being bullied."

In class, the bees are aimless.

During recess, the bees turn tornadoes of dust and leaves.

Some days the bees are melancholic. Someone spills soda in the hallway and the bees spend hours with sugar on their feelers, leaving small sticky footprints up the spines of #2 pencils. I'm not convinced they'll ever handwrite an essay. I'm not convinced they'll ever keep their hand-formation to themselves. I'm not sure this pre-reading vocabulary the ELL teacher had me prepare for them is even being read. I toss around on my sister's apartment couch at night and soon the sun comes up.

I make tea in a mug I found in the teacher lounge sink. It wasn't clean. Now my tea tastes like peppermint-tomato-soup. Now the fridge sounds like it's full of bees. Now I'm seeing a very old photo of my ex-husband on my Tinder account. Now I have to breathe and go to work.

+

One day I bring the bees an iPad. Even a bee can touch squares on a screen.

They land on all the letters at once. And what happens is – nothing.

+

I find one bee in my room after school. I'm not sure how long she's been there. I worry that she saw me scrolling through Facebook or Googling essential oils to keep anxiety at bay when I should have been grading. Her feelers are curled. She has four stripes on her body. She is trying to lift a pencil, and it's too much for her. I bring out the iPad, ask her to type her name.

Rome, she writes.

I ask her how school is going so far.

No, she writes.

"What do you want to talk about?" I ask. I sit down in my chair, and wheel myself closer to her. She is smaller than a penny. I wonder if she could even hold a penny up.

I am just one bee, she writes, zipping from letter to letter.

Not a queen, she writes.

A worker, she writes.

I'm supposed to pollinate flowers.

"Historically, that's true," I say, twisting the tie-neck of my blouse. She looks tired, zipping back and forth the keyboard like that, one letter at a time. "But it's such noble work you do. Honey bees are so important."

I'm part wasp, she writes.

"Oh," I say. I don't think it is physically possible to be both bee and wasp, but I don't want her to feel like I don't trust her. "Go on," I say.

I'm not interested in flowers, she writes.

I'm not interested in anything boring.

"Okay," I say. "But, what else can a honey bee do?" I regret it as soon as I say it. I can't believe I've just said it. I'm a teacher. Each student is an individual snowflake. Each bee in the swarm has a name.

If I were a younger teacher I wouldn't have said it.

If I were a younger teacher and had said it, I would have backtracked, I would have said, "That's the challenge the world is giving you, and the thing is, you need to challenge *back.*"

I'm looking at her and I can't tell if she's looking back at me.

Rome flies to the door, lands on the ground, and walks, on her hind legs, out.

+

Later at home, I learn these facts:

1. Honey is the only food that includes all the substances necessary to sustain life.
2. Honey bees have 6 legs, 2 compound eyes made up of thousands of tiny lenses, 3 simple eyes on the top of the head, 2 pairs of wings, a nectar pouch, and a stomach.
3. Their sense of smell is so precise that it could differentiate hundreds of different floral varieties and tell whether a flower carried pollen or nectar from meters away.
4. The honey bee's wings stroke incredibly fast, about 200 beats per second, thus making their famous, distinctive buzz.
5. A honey bee can fly for up to six miles, and as fast as 15 miles per hour.
6. A bee's brain is oval in shape and only about the size of a sesame seed.
7. The average worker bee produces about 1/12th teaspoon of honey in her lifetime.
8. Worker honey bees are female, live for about 6 weeks and do all the work.

I look at the calendar. It is the fifth week of spring.

+

At the start of class the next day, I use my most authoritarian teacher voice. “Rome,” I say. “I need to speak with you in the hallway.” I hold the door open for her and she zips out, landing on the spout of the drinking fountain.

I squat down and look at her in her five different eyes.

“I’m sorry,” I say. “About yesterday. About you not wanting to do something boring. I should have been listening.”

I reach into my purse and pull out a lemon candy. I rinse it in the drinking fountain so it’s not sticky. Rome inches across it, sucking up sweetness.

“We should go do something,” I say. “Where do you want to go? What do you want to be?”

I pull out my phone so she can write.

She writes, Once a bee uses its stinger, it dies.

She writes, It is estimated that 1100 honey bee stings are required to be fatal.

We are alone in the hallway. Inside my classroom, on the other side of the closed door, my students are already loud, already turning around in their seats and throwing paper airplanes and flicking erasers into the air. I can see Rome’s sisters swinging on the overhead lights.

“You’re right,” I say to Rome. “You’re special.”

I think of the woman I saw on the bees’ first day, their keeper, and how she unzippered her bag so they could go inside.

I open up my purse. Rome doesn’t hesitate. In she flies.

+

This bee is extraordinary, I think, as I'm escaping her away, as I'm sneaking out the side door of the school and zipping in my Corolla onto the interstate, towards who-knows-where-exactly, as the bee sleeps in my purse pocket near the lip-gloss and Tic-Tacs.

What's one bee? I think, feeling magnetized towards the pointy tops of mountains. In late fall, I've swept bees' bodies from back patios, their bodies light as corn flakes. I can't believe how different my life is in this moment: right *now.*

I drive and drive in curlicues.

When my boss calls, I ignore it.

He texts me EMERGENCY and WHERE RU?

I ignore, ignore. I toss my phone into the back. I imagine him having to cover my classes, and this makes me smile – my boss fumbling with a chalkboard and an overhead projector and 28 children and a swarm of 40 bees. I pull over on a scenic outlook, where the light crashes against one side of the mountain and darkens the other, where the air is thick with blue and a smattering of white clouds.

I kill the engine.

I can't hear anything, not even the hum of Rome.

I check Facebook and my ex-husband has a new profile picture of a duck wearing a football helmet. *That is so like him,* I think. *Hiding behind pictures of ducks.*

I step out of the car and open my purse. It's cooler up here, almost frosty. Rome flies out.

I hold out my phone so she can talk to me.

Cold, she writes, tiptoeing.

"I know," I say. I open my foundation clasp with a cushion inside. "This is warm," I tell her, and she chews off a corner and makes herself the tiniest cap. Six tiny bee-sized gloves.

I pull out a flask of whiskey from another purse pocket and wet my finger with a drop of it. "Here, this should help," I say, hoping it won't kill her. Rome licks my fingertip. I can almost perceive it. I take a sip of the whiskey, too, just enough to taste it.

"I'm so getting fired," I tell her. I'm feeling younger already, feeling the mountain wind blowing back my skirts. Feeling the washing-away feeling of not giving a single fuck. I say to Rome, "I just wanted to make a difference."

I have maybe four days left to live, she writes.

She writes, I haven't pollinated a single flower.

It's on principal, she writes.

"You aren't like other bees," I tell her. "Other bees would have huddled together to create heat in this cold, and instead you made a hat. Instead you are a singularity."

I am not, she writes, like anyone else on earth.

+

We decide she should go to space. There are no flowers in space. There is no nectar to collect. Plus, there is a launch scheduled pretty soon.

"How fast can you fly?" I ask.

So fast, she writes.

I pull a map out from the glove compartment in my car. The launch pad is not too far. Maybe 20 miles. The astronauts launch tomorrow. We've been talking about it in class for days.

"No bee has ever been to space," I say. "Spiders and jellyfish and dogs, but no bees."

What if I get scared and sting someone, she types.

"You? Scared?" I say.

I like whiskey, she writes. I can see why you brought it.

I pull the flask back out and unscrew the lid. "There's a little left. But it will make you slower."

She zips to the lip of the flask, and then she buzzes to my lip, and I can perceive her resting her head on my mouth for a moment, her whole body vibrating. Her wings blur, creating a small breath of air against my cheek. I close my eyes to focus only on that feeling.

"Do something extraordinary, Rome," I say.

And then Rome flies away. I open my eyes, and already she's barely a speck, whizzing down the mountain and away at what seems much faster than 15 miles per hour.

I wish I could read her thoughts.

I wish I could send her a text.

I wish she knew my number so she could tell me something from inside the ship.

+

Rome

The stars scatter across my vision like pollen on a windshield. At the launch pad, I hide in the soft hairs on the back of the astronaut's neck, but once we're in space, I let go. To let go: to fly without even beating my wings. I hover by the astronaut's ear. I can smell the spearmint shampoo the astronaut used this morning, her last shower before space. I smell agave from her breath. I smell the stars: a bright, metallic sting.

What are stars if not thousands of tiny, light-filled bees?

Down below, on earth, is the swarm. Fizzing across math-books. Gathering pollen from the goldenrods on the playground. I wonder if we'll all die at the same time, at the stroke of six weeks, all forty-one of us.

I wonder if time will move differently for me now that I am in space, if flying against the rotation of the earth will confuse my inner biology.

How long can a bee exist in space alone?

I'm not just a bee, I remind myself. I'm something more.

Outside the window of the space ship, Earth is a milky, blue ball. It looks so small from this height. I place my antenna against the glass and block the whole planet out of my sky.

Story Cube

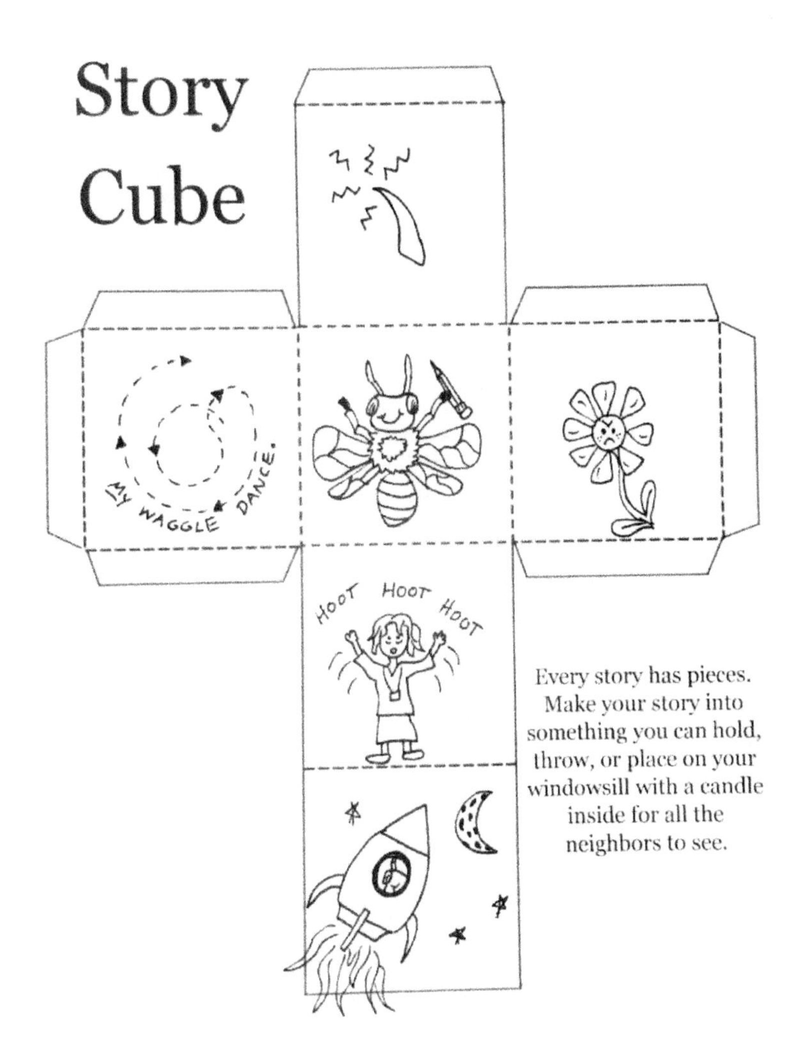

Every story has pieces. Make your story into something you can hold, throw, or place on your windowsill with a candle inside for all the neighbors to see.

OF ALL THE INFINITE POSSIBILITIES

The topic is prehistoric humans and their place in the food chain.

It says so right in the substitute lesson plan. Highlighted in yellow and underlined. Well shoot, I think. I'd hoped I'd be teaching something I already knew a lot about. Like how many glasses of milk you shouldn't drink in a row because you might die. Or Tiny House realty. Or how it's almost as likely to die falling off a ladder as it is to die falling out of bed. Or the best place to get Boba tea in the city.

Turns out none of this is useful.

"You can call me Mr. Achery," I say. "Achery rhymes with 'bakery.'"

The students barely glance at me. Their eyes are caught on a prepositions poster of squirrels going *across, along, under, until, behind, below* a tree. Their eyes are caught on the hair-scrunchie of the girl next to them, on a pigeon sitting outside the window.

This is the challenge, to get students to take me seriously.

Because I am here to fill in the gaps.

Because I am temporary.

And they know it.

"You ever get that spooky feeling when something is flying overhead?" I ask, whooshing one hand above me, as per the Substitute Teacher Instructional notes. Apparently, the Permanent Teacher is a bit of a dramatist.

The Permanent Teacher's name is Mrs. Johansen. Rumor

is her husband was hit by a car riding his bike to work, that he's in the hospital getting his organs replaced. He is starting to recognize shapes, they say in the teacher's lounge. They half-grin at me and hit the button on the one working Keurig machine.

I fumble with Mrs. Johansen's notes, not sure what to say next. Mrs. Johansen has written clearly at the top of the notes, *Engage the students. History has to feel real for them to get it.*

"You ever have that feeling when the hairs on your back raise?" I say. "When your stomach drops like an anchor—do you know what I mean?"

My temporary 4th graders are polite enough to nod.

I am watching their eyeballs for the gleam of engagement. I am trying not to notice the kid in the front row picking his nose, or the girl gnawing at her thumbnail. I am trying not to think about how stupid it is to ride your bike to work when the statistics are completely against it. I am trying not about how the average age of bicyclists killed in car crashes is like 45 or something, how 88% of those killed are male. How you have a choice most of the time to do something safe or do something stupid.

I look at my 4th graders, some of whom are eating the erasers off their pencils.

And I decide to do what's stupid.

I ditch the lesson plan. I drop the whole huge stack of it in the recycling bin. This gets their attention. Backs straighten. They side-glance one another. I ask the class, "Has anyone ever traveled back in time?"

No one answers, but their eyes stick on me.

"Please stand up and push in your chairs," I say, and they do.

Then I lead them outside to my time-machine.

+

I don't remember any of the substitute teachers from when I was a kid. I want to be different. I want to be memorable. I want to be the substitute teacher that kids write about in their college applications or that trends on YouTube because of the unique handshake he invents for each individual child. I have fantasies about one of my students reaching out to me twenty years from now and saying, "Mr. Achery, you're the reason I became a neurosurgeon." Or, "Mr. Achery, I didn't think I'd ever amount to anything until I met you. Now, would you believe it, I'm in the process of discovering a cure for the common cold."

Once, when I shared my teaching fantasies with my boyfriend, he suggested that maybe I got into teaching for the wrong reasons. He accused me of trying to be a Dead Poet Society teacher, and I took this as a cue to dress preppier: striped ties, starched shirt, blue sweater.

I have never been a memorable person. I'm cautious. Meticulously normal. My boyfriend calls this my superpower, that I'm incredibly generic. My haircut. My clothes. The rules I do and don't abide by. The words I use in sentences.

"So, you think I'm...boring?"

"You're welcome to surprise me," he said, smiling.

When I grew unhappy as an accountant, he wasn't surprised. He wasn't surprised when I looked into subbing, or when I traded in my car for the exact same model but several years newer. Wasn't surprised I found comfort in the *What is a ______ Grader Anyway?* series I stumbled upon online, or the way I was waiting at the door at 8 PM because that's when Amazon promised the books would be delivered by.

He was, however, surprised by the time machine.

He shook his head. "Wow, Greg. Seriously?"

That look – how he didn't know what to make of me – made my heart palpitate. He helped me move the time machine into the garage. "I always thought a time machine would be heavier," he said.

The time machine became a sort of joke in our house. Mostly my boyfriend forgot it was there, but every now and then he'd notice it in the corner of the garage and roll his eyes and ask, "How's the past treating you?" I laughed, but the jokes make me uncomfortable. I took to storing the time machine in the trunk of my car when I wasn't using it.

What my boyfriend doesn't realize is that it *works*. That I've stepped into our futures before. That in one possible future, I've seen us, necks looser and earlobes droopier, move to Texas and become ironic cattle ranchers. That I've felt how punishingly hot it is, hot enough to see mirages. That I know one day, in one future, I'll leave him, my boyfriend on a lonesome hill, me on horseback.

He has no idea.

+

"Walk in a straight line. Don't walk on the curb," I warn my temporary students as we walk through the parking lot. I tell the front office that we're going outside to examine rocks, which isn't exactly a lie.

I'm ready to watch their faces for that change. That new register, when they see me as more than what I appear.

My time machine looks like one of those metal detectors you pose inside at the airport. It is collapsible. It has many knobs and buttons. I pull it from the trunk of the car and set it in the gravel of the parking lot. I spin one of the knobs to "Prehistory."

I turn to my class. I can tell they're curious, but they're trying hard to hide it. "Today," I say to them. "I'm shaking things up. Now when we go back in time, two things are very important. One, listen to my directions. And two," here I smile at them, "have fun."

One by one, we walk through my time-machine, and *zip, ping, blip*. We're ten thousand years ago.

When we exit we are not in a parking lot, but inside a wide-mouthed and low-ceilinged cave. I dip my head around the stalactites, turn to watch the students, the star-shapes in their eyes. Their hands on their cheeks *Home Alone* style. "What the...?" a kid says. I can't stop grinning.

I am going to be the best temporary teacher they've ever had.

I kick away some rocks and debris and clear a space on the ground where my students can sit. I wipe down a cave wall with the end of my sleeve. Underneath the dust are images, and I think, What luck! What are the chances!? I'd planned on using the wall to scrawl terminology, but this is much better.

I act like I knew the cave drawings would be here. "These, class," I say, "are examples of primary cave documents. Can you tell me what you see here?"

"It's a picture of a woolly mammoth!" one kid shouts out, and I thank him but remind the class that they should raise their hands, because too much shouting might cause a rock fall in a cave like this.

"I see a bird. A big bird with talons," offers the girl closest to me.

"Looks bigger than any bird I've ever seen," says another

student. He points to a little stick figure that I think must be a cave-person, underneath the drawing of the bird. "See! It must be HUGE!"

"Cave art can tell us a lot about the life of prehistoric societies," I tell them, and remembering the topic of the day, add, "What do these drawings tell you about a human's place in the food chain?"

But none of the 4th graders want to talk about that. Instead, they are asking me questions I don't know the answers to, like, "Are these paintings made from blood? And how much blood? And is it HUMAN?"

I am the teacher and I don't like being wrong, so I guess, "Yes! Undoubtedly!" Then I lower my voice and lean into it. "These are blood drawings," I say, "and it's time to go scavenging. After cave art, the best way to learn about the food chain is by examining bones."

"What kind of bones?" they want to know, and I say, "Any kind."

I break them into teams, and they slink off in pairs and go roaming the cave.

+

I never took education courses, but I do frequent a Teacher Supply Store, where all the employees are cheery as glass about to break, lemonade smiles and voices like plush robes.

Once, a smiley woman in a dress dotted with limes found me in the Geography aisle, and I got so nervous I bought three wipe-down posters of lions reading, and lions wearing lab goggles, and lions holding protractors in their teeth. But when I got home, I realized I had nowhere to put them, because I'm not a real teacher, I'm a substitute, something temporary. I have no walls or windows or floor.

My 4th graders come back with all sorts of things: bones and sticks and rocks carved into points. No one's found a skull. But one girl, who introduces herself as Mollie, found a tooth. She holds it up proudly and bares her teeth for comparison. "How big is it?" she asks. "Is it bigger than mine?"

I tell Mollie she'll get a prize when we're back in class. Then I ask my students to gather back around. I say, "The light in the cave is turning orange, so it must be nearly what class?"

None of them get when I am asking for.

"Sunset," I say, alone.

I feel clammy. I feel like a clam. This is the first time I've brought anyone in the time machine with me, and I didn't realize how much I'd been aching to share it until now.

I say, "Let's venture out from the cave and explore. Let's see what else we can gather about early humans. Remember, this is *pre*history. Before history." I wiggle my finger in the air for emphasis. "This is before we had the language to write stories down." Before I'm halfway through my sentence, my 4th graders have vamoosed. They rush out the mouth of the cave into the twilight, the forest thick, buzzing, autumnal, the trees stretched large and clinging to their colors. I throw my neck back in wonderment. My voice is starting to tire. I wonder if I've fulfilled the state standards for history yet. I wonder if this is what it's like – success.

My 4th graders are throwing themselves into piles of leaves, sneezing so hard they tumble backwards, wrestling their way up ancient tree trunks. I sneak back into the cave and start warming up the time machine, so we can get back to school in time for lunch, and when I return outside, there's not a 4th grader to be seen.

+

What is a Fourth Grader Anyway? is Crayola bright and pocket-sized and has a tiny cartoon of a child on a spring-coil, launching himself up. Towards...enlightenment? I puzzled over the cover with my boyfriend, and he laughed at the chapter titles: Girl Drama Begins, What to Do About the Bathroom, Sometimes *Everything* Goes Wrong, Writing Emails is Like Making a Sandwich.

This is what I reach for when my 4th graders disappear off the earth.

When the nerves in my body start to make me feel like my skin is unzipping.

I tell myself, they're not disappeared off the earth.

I tell myself, Calm Down, Greg. Take a chill pill. Take a Xanax.

I keep thinking the words *liable, irresponsible, negligent,* and it makes a jail-door sound.

I walk through the trees. I don't know many of my temporary students' names, so I just call, "Fourth Graders!" I climb a short tree with low branches to try to get a better vantage point, but all I can see is more trees holding up the sky. It is wide and purple and orange and the biggest sky I've seen.

A large shadow passes overhead and the hairs on my neck stand up. I am getting that feeling like my stomach is an anvil.

I try breathing. I try to remember the YouTube tutorial on panic attacks, on grounding.

I think about the sound of my boyfriend sleeping, or a pile of folded sweaters, or room temperature butter, or other things that calm me down.

I breathe deeply, thinking if I can get calm enough, things can go back to how they were. My students will be OK. I will be normal and boring and good.

The shadow above me has wings.

It descends.

+

I've gone to the future dozens of times. Just quick looks. You're not supposed to walk around inside your own future. According to the instructions that came in the box, you could catch a disease or mess things up. You can do the same things in the past, but the future feels more delicate because we just don't know about it yet.

I've seen my boyfriend marry me.

Cheat on me.

Remarry me.

Plant hydrangeas with me.

Fall off a ladder.

Drown in a lake.

Gallop as cattle ranchers.

Lavish ourselves in Tokyo.

Cry when it's me in the lake, one time, drowning.

Every single time it's different.

A couple days ago, my boyfriend announced over dinner that I was acting very weird. Had been acting weird for weeks. "You've been," he paused, "unpredictable." I laughed. I told him I didn't know what he meant. But once he was asleep, I slipped back out of the bed and into the garage, tinkering with the dials, looking into twenty, thirty, forty years from now.

To figure out which choices, which seemingly small decisions, would cause which futures.

+

By the time I process that the shadow is a bird, an enormous, mammoth eagle, it is too late to duck. Too late to climb back down the tree.

The eagle grasps me under the arms and lifts. The ground falls away. My right shoulder is bleeding, and every breath is pain. The eagle huffs and flies vertically like she is swimming.

We must be up miles. The forest below has changed from being individual trees to one single blob of green.

Then, I realize we're approaching something. A cliff-face. A cliff-face that a fall from such heights would be certain death.

The eagle unclenches me into a giant nest. I roll, scrape my knees. When I stop rolling, I try to get to my feet. I brace one hand against the puncture wound on my shoulder. My clip-on tie slips off. The nest is barbarous sticks and peat and grass, two large eagle's eggs in the center. At first, there are no signs of my 4th graders. Then I spot Mollie, crouching behind one of the eggs. I'm relieved to see her, and then terrified. The eagle steps into the forefront of my vision. The eagle, making a ceiling over me. The eagle, opening his wings. The eagle, cocking his head at me, staring at me from the side. All these moments, I think, pulling them in like a collection. It's weird how much can happen, and how slow it is, before I die.

I want to pick up a rock or something, but there isn't a rock.

So I pick up what is in front of me.

I lift the eagle's egg.

The eagle, she's watching me.

She feels like a she now that the egg is in my arms.

Mollie crawls forward enough to touch my sock, to warn me, but the egg is already high in my arms. Whatever's inside is almost completely formed. My 4th graders are all here. I can see them now, peeping behind the rim of the nest. I try not to lose my strength, try to remember anything I can about yoga or body building or air. I breathe through the nose, out through the mouth.

"Eyes on me," I roar. And I realize they are.

The eagle rears back and I spread myself out in an X. There is a man buried inside of me, underneath the meticulous outside, a prehistoric-me, an unruly me, full of muscle and instinct, and the havoc of listening to him, the havoc of his arms in my arms—

I thrust the egg.

I chuck it *hard*.

I conk that eagle right in the chest, and the egg bounces into the air, and I can see her heart lurch after it. The eagle dives downward off the mountain.

And we hastily make our escape.

+

It takes us two days to hike back down the mountain to the forest floor, clinging to the thickets, sleeping under trees. I stay up all night keeping watch and my students are well-behaving. I have only minor discipline problems. We eat grass and some acorns. We're so hungry we all get a little loopy. I think my students are whispering about me behind my back, or maybe it's just the murmuring of the leaves. One of the boy students goes missing for enough time to make me think the eagle's gotten him, but then he comes back holding two dead mice in his fist. I don't have the heart to tell him we haven't invented fire yet.

We drink spring water clear as blue eyes. I don't let them soak their toes for too long in case of unknown creatures lurking beneath the surface. I make them memorize the spelling of hypothermia and pneumonia, though I forget exactly what each of those words mean and what makes them different.

"Tomorrow, when we get back to class," I say, planting the belief firmly in their brains, "we'll have a spelling bee. And an illustration contest. And learn Roman Numerals. I hope you've been paying attention," I say.

If I pretend authority, if I pretend know-how, my 4th graders won't notice that I don't know.

I say, "You'll use this the rest of your life." I use great gestures, the jaunt of my elbow, my rusted-open eyes.

I shake my *What is a 4th Grader Anyway?* booklet at them. The pages rustle loose.

We break for lunch, though we don't have anything to eat. One boy, claiming to be a Boy Scout, tells us we can eat the inner bark of some pine trees. He scratches at the bark of an evergreen and uses a rock to splinter off some chunks of white wood.

"I can't be sure of this species, though," he says. "It's possible it's toxic."

A few of the students are hungry enough to take a piece anyway. They chew at the bark like it's gum and make faces but don't spit it out.

We're just about to continue on, when Mollie announces, "This looks familiar. I remember seeing these sorts of trees around the cave. Maybe that means we're close."

"Yes! Very astute, Mollie," I exclaim. "You just earned yourself another prize!"

Overhead a shadow passes.

We all crouch low in the forest. We press our bodies against the earth. We wait. The shadow circles, circles, passes.

My students get to their feet before I do, and so for a few seconds that feel like a few minutes, I stay on my belly, watching them through the grass. They dust off their knees. They tuck their hair behind their ears. Then they keep walking. My 4th graders move as a herd, as a flock. They move in the same direction without speaking.

+

I think of one of the futures I saw through the time machine. The future where I leave him on a horse. How could I leave him on a horse? I kept wondering, obsessively. And I needed to see what happened, after. I saw my boyfriend sitting alone on the front steps of a porch. Dark rimmed glasses, silver hair combed back, knees bony through his jeans. The land speckled with cattle and cacti. The sun low-slung, turning everything red. He was smiling, in a quiet, content sort of way I knew well. I longed to see myself emerge from the house, carrying two mugs of tea, or maybe cranberry juice. Whatever old people drank. I longed to see my silhouette on the horizon, myself old and on horseback, galloping back. But that me never emerged, and eventually I realized. I wasn't coming back. My boyfriend was alone in this future, and he was happy.

At the time, this future filled me with fear. I returned through the time machine back to the garage, storming, baffled, furious at myself, furious at that smile, furious at all the god-knows-what that led us there.

But here, now, my body is dampening in prehistoric mud. I imagine letting my body sink further into the mud, letting my skin and muscle and fat enter the food chain, letting the earth fossilize whatever's left.

I think of my boyfriend silver-haired and happy.

I think of my body in the desert, how I must have fallen off the horse on the way back to him, how I must have ended up bones. Why else would I have left him?

"Mr. Achery!" I hear a student call. "Look!"

I'll get up in a moment. I can see it already: me following my students' voices through the trees. The open, waiting mouth of a cave. My students' hands on the time machine already, guessing at the knobs. But for now, I stay here, where I am.

Hypothesis: Time is linear.

Complete the timeline below.

Secondary hypothesis: Time is not linear.

It is…circular? Spiraled? Triangular? Multi-faceted?

Draw time as you see it in the space provided below.

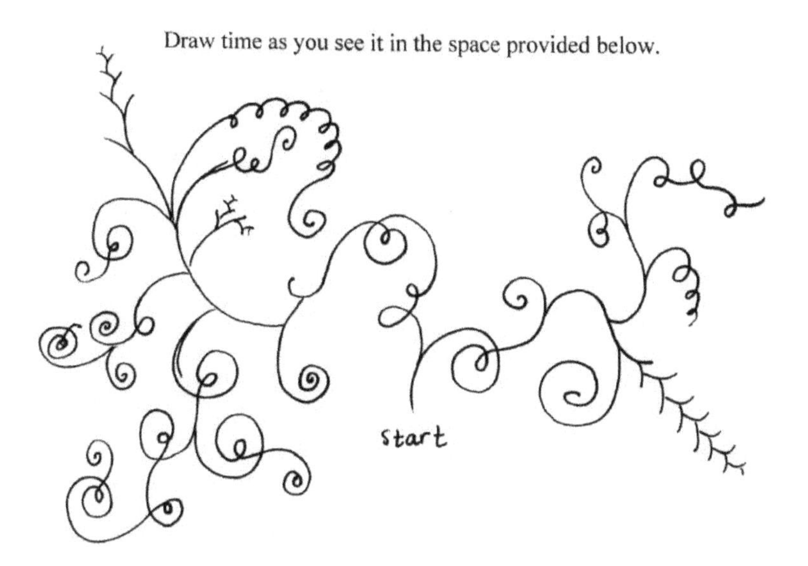

THE GIRL WHO TURNS TO RABBITS

When we get nervous we turn into white rabbits. We get put into a white room.

+

Sometimes it doesn't happen all at once. I can tell I'm getting nervous when whiskers poke out on my cheeks, when my ears stretch-grow under my hair, pointing upward and swiveling like radio antennae. I know it's happening when I can hear pencils sharpening three classrooms over, when I can smell the cafeteria on the first floor of the school frying bacon. But usually it starts in my heart. For me it does. It's a spilling of rice grains, or a necklace of firecrackers, or my heart is full of mousetraps – that's what it feels like.

Sometimes it does happen all at once – one moment I don't understand who Ulysses S. Grant is, and I see the word TEST on the whiteboard, and I write in my assignment notebook in red bubble letters over and over and then poof, I'm a white rabbit with a red pen clenched in my teeth, and I'm seeing the world out the sides of my head.

+

I say "we turn into white rabbits," because it happens to a lot of us here: The School for Gifted and Nervous White Rabbits. When we graduate, we're supposed to have mastered it – we're supposed to have gripped our kicking, squirming hearts and held them shut like a compact. Our hearts are supposed to be solid as a turtle shell – with the soft thing hidden within. If we can't control it, we don't graduate. We can't leave until we've gone years without turning into white rabbits.

I feel like I will never graduate. Sometimes I turn into not just one white rabbit, but many. The more nervous I am, the more white rabbits I turn into. I slide down the hallways, scatter through doorways, but they always catch me, all of me, white-gloved and white-suited. Then, they take me to the white room.

+

The thing about the white room is: it's awful. It's designed to dissuade us from using our powers to turn into white rabbits. In the white room, we panic. It feels like the walls are all muzzles, and behind the muzzles are teeth. I have teeth too, and I use them, running buckeyed and brainless through the room, teeth barred, a foam of white fur in my mouth. The floor is soft with the fur of past white rabbits. Sometimes we're shedding and sometimes we're tearing into or torn. The walls are white-rabbit white, the ceiling is a rectangle of sun, so blinding there are no shadows. There is nowhere to hide.

Once in the white room, I close my eyes. You're not supposed to do this as a rabbit – it's very dangerous as a rabbit to close all 3 of your eyelids, to pull the wooly one down. We learn about all this in school. We learn about our rabbit teeth growing into painful points, about the sensitive pads of our feet, about how we are poor swimmers and territorial lovers – all the things we learn to dissuade us from becoming white rabbits. I am trying. I have been told to breathe and so I am trying it: breathing. I am trying to picture the ocean, trying to feel like I will not be a failure forever, even though I cannot picture what that looks like. I imagine foam. I imagine a seagull scooping me up. I try to picture being buried underground, my fur decomposing, my little white bones. I try picturing how quiet it is down there with the tree roots.

+

This is the only way I know how to not turn into white rabbits. I think of my little white bones and I think of the roots of plants and the soundlessness of earthworms and of a place without teeth. I close my eyes and I stop my feet from running and I think: one day I'll be bones. Even if I'm always white rabbits, even if I learn to control it: I will end up bones. I'm okay with ending up bones.

+

My sister doesn't turn to white rabbits. My sister turns to a lion. My sister turns to a lion and sometimes my sister, she eats white rabbits. She has promised to never eat me, that she would recognize me by my smell, that she knows the difference between my white rabbits and the white rabbits she likes to eat.

She goes to a different school, of course, The School for Gifted and Angry Lions, but she is the type of student who scales fences in a single bound. She is the type of student who causes mischief and vandalism, or that's what her school calls it when we are missing white rabbits, when our attendance steeply drops in the night.

+

In between our schools is jungle. In the jungle is where the wild children live.

We can hear them through our windows. It isn't safe out there. The wild children turn to animals and never turn back. They don't want to go to school. They don't want to turn back.

+

In the jungle, the boys turn into snakes. The girls turn like a wish into thorns, into thistle, into a Venus flytrap. The boys turn into vultures and the girls turn into cats, narrow and yellow-eyed. Don't go into the jungle they tell us at the School for Gifted and Nervous Rabbits. GO INTO THE JUNGLE they bellow and stomp at lion basketball games, lion football games, lion pep rallies. At the School for Gifted and Nervous Rabbits, we play Scrabble pretty competitively. We learn printmaking. We iron. We have lettuce-tossing competitions where the whole school goes mad.

+

One night a lion appears in my room. I had been running around as white rabbits because, see, the thing about me is I don't just turn into rabbits when I'm nervous. I turn into rabbits when I'm giddy. I had been racing around my bedroom carpet at top speed, so quickly I charged up with static. When a lion appears through the window weeping, a lion I know is my sister, I try to turn human again. I try to calm down and use all the breathing techniques I've learned, but I'm still a rabbit. My sister touches her nose to mine, and I shock her. I hop up onto my bed and try to look as human as I can by leaning against my pillow.

It's weird seeing a weeping lion. My sister is only supposed to turn to a lion when she gets angry. I never get angry, and so I never turn to a lion. I always thought people were supposed to turn to slugs when they got sad, but this is no slug. This is a lion with tears round as pearls, this is a lion with long cry-lines flattening the folds in her mane. She has a mane like a male lion, and it is as orange-gold as a canyon. I reach my rabbit paws up to her eyes. I have to do this sideways so I can see her, sideways, so I know if her jaw is going to clench around my neck. I'm nervous. I lift a paw, pet her cheek.

What's wrong, Lion? I ask.

Rabbit, she says, I hate myself.

You hate yourself?

I hate myself, says the lion. She says, I can't do anything right. I'm always a lion. I'm always angry.

My rabbit legs are shaking. I can see her glistening, white teeth. So much bigger than mine. You are a great lion, I say.

You think I'm going to eat you. My own sister thinks I'm going to eat her.

I think everyone's going to eat me, I say. I'm always scared.

She says, I'm always angry.

I say, I love that you are angry. I wish I were like you.

She picks me up in her lion jaws, her jowls wet with tears. She picks me up by my torso, so she can feel that rattle-can heart of mine, the little self-detonator I keep in my chest. She jumps from the window and lands lightly, me safe against her tongue.

She carries us to the jungle between our two schools.

With one paw, she digs me a burrow. She drops me down and I bound into it, digging hard to make it longer, wider, deeper, closer to the roots of the earth.

+

Underground, in the jungle, there are many of us now. The girls who turn to white rabbits.

+

We build the warren ourselves.

There are multiple entrances for quick escape.

We build nests of our own fur.

Our young are small and blind, born in the middle of the night. By morning, they are warm and round-bellied. Their eyes are little wells filled with light.

We feel the walls of our home with our whiskers.

We bear and we bear and we bear.

The School for Gifted and Nervous White Rabbits

Application Materials

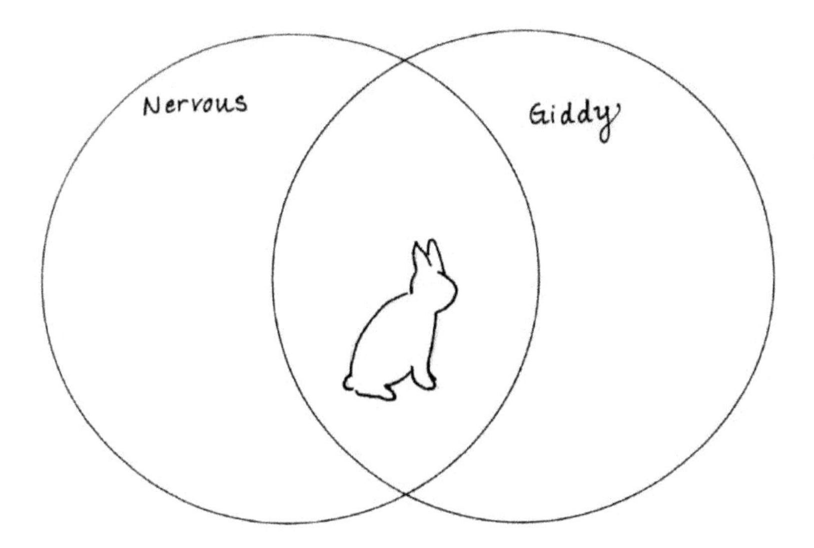

THE BOY WHO TURNS TO TOADS

When I drop out, I go where all the drop-outs go. The jungle is full of beasts with teeth, but at least there are no detentions, no pop quizzes, no ink smudges trailing down wrists, no teachers locking me in quiet rooms.

My first night as a drop-out, I turn into a plague of toads. I balloon my neck taut and bellow at the walls of the School for Insecure and Underfoot Woodland Creatures. I bellow all night. I make sure no one sleeps. I urinate on the freshly cut lawn. I burrow holes in the zinnia gardens. A barn owl eats one of me, but I don't care, because there are so many of me.

I think, This is it. I'll never have to be human again. No more algebra, no more locked doors, no more being in one skin when I could be in many.

+

The teachers said I have an insecurity problem. They told me that I didn't like my human body. They told me that I didn't raise my hand enough in class. They told me that that is why I turn into creatures that hide in mud at the bottom of ponds and flatten their bodies under heavy grey stones. When they found me crawling in the showers, puddling my body under the spray of the showerheads or splatting myself against the tiled walls, they would gather me in nets built to catch butterflies, take me to the Panic Room until I turned human again.

For homework, every student was supposed to do confidence building exercises. We were each provided with a full-length mirror. For twenty minutes every night, we were instructed to stand naked in front of the mirror with our arms raised in a victory pose. The pose was supposed to trick our brains into believing we were victorious. "Victorious like a lion?" we'd say. "Victorious like a hawk?" But the teachers dissuaded us from using such similes. "Victorious like a human," they'd say.

+

I thought I'd never have to be human again once I entered the jungle of drop-outs.

I'm surprised when the morning after I dropped out, I wake at the base of a banyan tree naked and fleshy and with only one pair of eyelids. My skin goosepimples with nakedness. I cover myself with my hands. The jungle is dark even though it's daytime. The light filtering through the canopy leaves is swampy. I feel for the part of me that the barn owl ate last night and find it: a hollowness under my kneecap, a loss I could live with.

I set out to find the other drop-outs, the other wild children, the ones the teachers warned us changed into animals and never changed back. I imagine them living in a hollow tree like Lost Boys, giraffes and peacocks and beavers and mastiffs coexisting in their wildness.

All day I look for them. Poison ivy rashes up my bare thighs, my feet blacken and blister. Sometimes I catch glimpses of bodies between the leaves. A plume of blue feathers, an explosion of antlers, a bowed tusk. I call out to them, thunder through the underbrush with my clumsy human feet, and they disappear.

When I get tired, I sit on my knees on a fallen log. I close my eyes. I listen for the *pat-pat-pat* of my heart's chambers condensing from four to three, reach for the bubble in my throat that grows and grows until it chokes me. These are the signs that I am about to turn into toads. At school, I practiced this in my dorm room in the early morning when I knew the hall monitors had fallen asleep at their posts. If I wanted it enough, I could turn into toads in thirty seconds flat. It was like all day I'd been holding the toads back, and turning was as easy as unclenching my fist.

Now, though, I can't feel the toads. My heart is big and wet. My throat is dry. My stomach growls with human hunger.

I open my eyes. I think of a girl from school who could turn into a line of ants just by breathing. She was the only student I knew who would change only when she wanted to. She didn't change in the middle of improv lessons when she tripped over a mic cord and we all snorted into our elbows. She didn't change when she got her period during gym class and we all saw the spot of crimson grow against the baby blue cotton of her shorts.

The girl who turned into ants spent more time in the Panic Room than any of us, because the teachers knew that when she changed, it was always because she meant to.

The girl who turned into ants would never turn into a queen ant: fat and fed and worshipped. She'd only turn into the worker ants: small and strong and dispensable. She sat in front of me in Social Studies. Her hair was brown and uncombed. I didn't think much about her then, but I think about her now. If I was toads and she was ants, all of me would eat all of her up.

+

Everyone's Panic Room is different. In my Panic Room, there were no corners. In my Panic Room, even the ceiling was round. And on the walls, heat lamps like panting mouths. Red hot, unrelenting. They prickled my skin dry. They made me hop in circles, hop myself bruised. I tried to turn myself into stones that I could hide beneath, but I didn't work that way.

+

When I'm a toad, I have memories that don't belong to me. Frosty winter dreams of my blood crystalizing in my chest, my body becoming mud. Wet, slippery, tailed memories of sliding through puddles, my body indistinguishable from my brothers', algae filling my mouth, the taste of green. Memories of yellow teeth, curled talons, sharp beaks. Memories passed down to me like pebbles.

+

In the middle of the darkest part of the jungle, I find a black pond covered in giant, rimmed lily pads as wide as I am tall. It's not a large pond, and I wonder how I've managed to find it. I hope that it isn't a coincidence. I hope that it is the part of me that is always toad drawing me to the water. I hope this means I'll be able to change again.

I am feeling painfully hungry. The pain creeps into my throat and behind my eyes. It makes me dizzy, it makes my vision shimmer. Mosquitoes hover like smoke over the water. If I was a toad, I'd zip-snatch them into my belly. But as a human, they eat me. Red bumps rise on my arms and my only consolation is that the bumps make me feel almost toady.

At school, we learned that if you act victorious, you will become victorious. If you act like a human who can't turn into woodland creatures, you become a human who can't turn into woodland creatures.

+

All night, I try this process in reverse.

I leap from the grassy bank onto one of the giant lily pads. It wobbles. Ripples spread across the pond, creating a domino-effect of small creatures hopping from the banks into the water. The lily pad remains afloat. I crouch on its smooth surface, my knees at my shoulders, my fingers outstretched.

Act an animal, and become an animal, I tell myself.

I dive into the pond. The water is soupy and warm. It fills my ears and my eyes and I let it, whooshing the air from my lungs in a stream of bubbles so I sink, sink until the mushy pond bottom is in my palms. I try to grasp it like a blanket, and it slips between my fingers. I reach again, find a knot of seaweed. And something hard. Maybe a branch or maybe a skeleton, the skeleton of a frog that didn't bury itself deep enough in the winter and froze in the middle of a dream.

I wait for the drowning to start. The human body will always force itself to breathe, to inhale, even against its will. A last ditch effort to survive. A toad can hold its breath for four to six hours underwater. Humans can hold their breaths for, on average, two minutes.

But I'm not changing. White firecrackers burst in the corners of my vision. I kick and kick until my head breaks the surface of the pond and then I breathe with croaking breaths, still just one of me.

+

I chew on a handful of grass. I lick morning dew from a fern. I watch a string of carpenter ants march up a gumtree.

+

On my fifth day as a drop-out, I return to the edge of the jungle. I sit in the shadows, where no one can see me.

I'm still not toads.

I watch the school's walls change from gray to pink to black as the sun sets.

There is one thing I want. I want to talk to her, the girl who can turn into ants.

I wait until the moon is high and all of the windows are dark, and then I stand and step out of the jungle and onto the lawn. For the first time in days, my feet move easily. The moon turns my skin gray. I feel my nakedness, bumpy and boney all over.

It is easy to find an open window. I hoist myself into an empty classroom and shut the window behind me. I pad down the smooth, cool hallways. I pull down a curtain in a common room and wrap it around myself like a towel.

I climb the spiral staircase to the dorms. Quiet. I'd forgotten how quiet it is here.

I find her room and test the knob. Unlocked. We aren't allowed to lock our doors at night so the monitors can check in on us, make sure we aren't changing in our sleep.

She sits up as I enter. I wonder if she heard me coming, or if she was already awake.

Who are you? she asks.

I'm afraid to turn on the lights, so I pull up her blinds to let in the moonlight. I see my reflection in the glass of the window and I am surprised by what I see, a creature that isn't human or animal, hair matted, all collarbones and chin.

Oh, she says.

Her hair is in a bun. She is wearing long, buttoned-up pajamas. Her blanket is folded neatly at the end of her bed, like she's never used it.

Sorry, I say. Sorry, I didn't mean to—

How is the jungle? she cuts me off.

I step away from the window, out of the moonlight. I've noticed my own stink, and I have this feeling that if she can't see me, she also won't be able to smell me.

I say to her, The jungle is full of creatures like me.

I want to explain that the forest of drop-outs is for those who don't want to control their inner animal. It's for those who like the feeling of letting go. The hardening along our spine threatening to calcify us. Our thumbs migrating down our wrists, shrinking into dewclaws. Vestigial body parts busting like fireworks from the places where our joints meet.

Instead I say, You don't even know who you are until you're out there. I say, I saw some ants and thought of you.

I tell her, I think you should come with me.

She is quiet. She sits up in bed. I notice that her bare toes are all exactly the same size and shape. They twitch against her sheets.

It's better in the jungle, I tell her. I can be toads all day.

I don't know why I'm lying, but the more I talk, the more her toes seem to twitch.

No one tells you how lonely it is to be human, I say. When you're human, there's only you. But when you're an animal, you are many yous. You have all of these memories and voices telling you the right way to be, keeping you company.

As I'm speaking, the girl who can turn into ants turns

into ants. She is a girl and then she is ants. She is many ants, all swarming together in a pile in the center of her bed, so dense and black that at first I think she's just a shadow.

I sit on the floor and watch her. Worker ants are lost without their queen. Is she lost? Whom does she follow?

If I was a little boy, I'd use a magnifying glass and the sun to burn her alive. If I was toads I'd eat her.

I wait for a toady hunger to grow in my gut, for my heart to shrink, for my body to turn into a plague of bodies.

I crawl into the bed. At first I crouch above the ants, and then I lower myself into them. They scatter like rippling water, then swarm back. An ebb and a flow. They crawl over my body, between my fingers, into my hair, into my ears, over my eyelids. I try not to breathe. I try to hear their quiet, quiet chatter.

Together, we will go into the jungle. The ants will teach me how to be toads again. In the jungle, there are tunnels, and places to rest, and places to burrow, and when wild rabbits and wild toads and wild ants join us, we'll make places to bear our young. Our young will be born, small and whole, in the middle of the night. Our young will be extensions of ourselves.

We will learn to love ourselves, and in loving, multiply.

Name ____________________

IT'S NOT A CIRCLE, IT'S A CHAIN

Food chains start with photosynthesis and end with decay. Consider your role in the food chain. Draw the food chain, using yourself as an element. Don't forget decay.

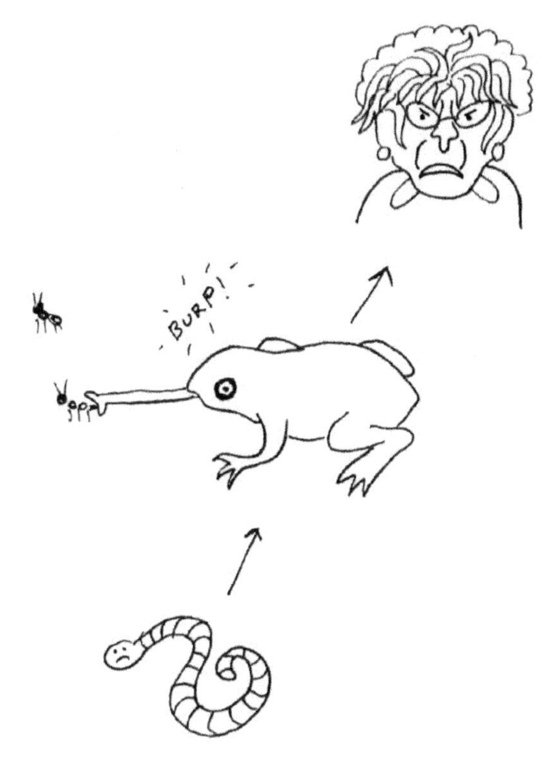

THE MASCOT

The teachers are in the break room sharing dirty theories about their school mascot, the Roadrunner.

Ms. Philips stirs chicken flavor into her Ramen and says, "He grabbed my ass once, when I was introducing the cheerleaders."

Mrs. Downton wonders if the Roadrunner is inhabited by the ghost of our school's founder.

Dr. Cherez suggests the Roadrunner lives in the rafters of the auditorium like the Phantom of the Opera.

Mr. Chuck thinks about this, and then adds, "Do you think he masturbates in there? Inside the costume, I mean."

"Gross, Chuck. Stop," several voices respond.

But Chuck just shrugs and coats his hands in hand sanitizer that fills the room with the sting of alcohol. Several teachers surreptitiously pinch their nostrils shut, count backwards from ten.

No one has ever seen the Roadrunner outside of his costume. No one knows if he is tall or short or beer-bellied or skeletal or mustached or clean shaven. The Roadrunner always leaves just before the end of an assembly, sprints through the double-doors of the gym into the hallway to applause and whoops, wings pumping to the beat of the pep band. Then the halls clog with students, chokes with bodies. The teachers are busy telling us to be "quiet foxes" in the hallways, urging lines straight, rescuing dropped trapper keepers. By the time they untangle themselves, the

Roadrunner is back in the broom closet, propped limply against the water heater amongst buckets and mops and the bags of kitty litter they use when one of their students hurls on the carpet.

Without a body in it, the Roadrunner is stiff and musty. Without a body in it, it still has mesh eye-pockets stiff as kneepads, feathers leather-thick. It's a large and rank cocoon, big and black on the inside.

"No one remembers hiring him," Mrs. Downton says. "He must have started working here before our time."

They imagine their Roadrunner, their Raving, Raging, Roaring Roadrunner, concealing the body of an old man. The firm mesh of the costume holds his decrepit body upright. In his day-to-day life, they imagine he hobbles on aching bunions, uses an electric scooter to move through Sam's Club. But when he places the felt Roadrunner mask over his shoulders, zips the torso up to his neck, he feels the pep return to his body, feels like he did as a boy running through his backyard at night, fingers only visible by the silhouettes they made against the stars.

+

Ms. Cardinal never speaks up during these break room gossip sessions. She stays quiet, Styrofoam cup of tea clasped between her palms, because Ms. Cardinal has a secret.

Between two and three times a week, she visits the Roadrunner's limp, lifeless body in the broom closet. She props a chair under the door knob, turns off the single hanging bulb, and feels her way through the dark to the Roadrunner. She lowers herself into its felt arms. The Roadrunner has a parted beak reinforced with a cardboard cone that has collapsed a little over the years and gives the

Roadrunner's face a drunk, lopsided look. But in the dark, it feels like the soft curve of a valley. The Roadrunner has a white downy belly and blue wings padded with cotton biceps. Ms. Cardinal likes to prop her cheek against the bicep or the chest and imagine she can hear a heartbeat. Sometimes she runs her hands over the feathers. Sometimes she strokes the plume. She can hear the muted din of student voices in neighboring classrooms, the hush after the stampede towards recess.

Most of the time, she talks. She whispers secrets into where she thinks the Roadrunner's ears should be (she looked it up once—birds have asymmetrical ear holes on the sides of their heads). She talks to the Roadrunner in a nearly soundless whisper, like a wife might speak to her husband in bed in the morning, trying not to wake the dog at their feet.

She likes to imagine the Roadrunner as a 65-year-old man, a simple man who is maybe a little shorter than her but makes up for it with broad shoulders and thick hands. Hands like an Amish farmer's, a man who picks roots with fists instead of machines. Of course, she imagines him quiet. Married once, a long time ago, to a beautiful doctor. One day, while saving a young boy's life in a highway accident—kneeling, on the shoulder, taking his pulse—a car skidded on some loose gravel and the beautiful doctor was struck. The Roadrunner never thought he could love again.

Ms. Cardinal nods to herself, satisfied with this story. Even though she teaches math, she still has a good imagination. She likes to think the Roadrunner is surprised, grateful for the late-in-life love he is finding with Ms. Cardinal.

"I know love is a strong word," she says to the Roadrunner before she leaves the broom closet. "You don't have to say it back."

+

The teachers have theories about Ms. Cardinal, too.

It's Tuesday morning, and they're huddled in the break room with mugs of coffee, trying to stretch out the minutes before first period with gossip.

Mr. Chuck says, "She has crushes on all of the football players. I hear she steals her favorite player's jersey at the end of every year and adds it to a shrine she keeps in her garage."

"She's just lonely," Mrs. Downton says kindly. "She missed her chance at finding a husband."

The door swings open, and Ms. Cardinal walks in. They watch her walk to the fridge and place a bagged lunch inside. She leaves without making eye contact with anyone.

Someone clears their throat.

"So, has anyone seen Martin Turner swim yet?" Mrs. Downton asks.

Martin is new to the school this year, and his team has had a winning season. He is rumored to be on track for the Olympics.

"Probably taking steroids," Mr. Chuck says, but this is the first time any team at the school has won anything, so no one responds.

The Important Swim Meet is next Saturday, and Martin's teachers have been careful to not assign much homework. They've kept the spelling list simple and water-related this week: chlorine, goggles, filter. They avoid bumping into Martin in the hallways, which is difficult, because his upper body is bull-like, boulder-like, enormous for a fifteen-year-old.

"How can someone that *big* swim so well?" Ms. Cardinal

mutters, placing her coffee mug in the sink.

She doesn't know that Martin Turner wonders the same thing, that Martin Turner used to be a wrestler at his old school until he was expelled for choking someone unconscious in a locker room fight, that Martin Turner didn't mean to be good at swimming when he came here – it was an accident. It was always an accident with Martin Turner.

+

Mr. Chuck is organizing a Pep Rally for after school on Friday. The cheerleaders have been asked to arrange a special water-themed cheer that will integrate the Roadrunner, the band will be playing a jazzy rendition of "Under the Sea," and the auditorium will be strung with blue streamers and paper fish.

Dr. Cherez hopes an American Olympics recruiter might be in town for the meet, and for the rest of the week, while they're teaching trigonometry or World War II or how to prevent STDs, the teachers daydream about a future where news reporters seek them out in parking lots, asking, "Did you always know Martin Turner would be a star?" "How does it feel to be *the* Martin-the-Star-Turner's favorite teacher?" They wonder if they'll tell the truth, that Martin was a perfectly polite boy with average grades, or if they'll make up a story about Martin's out of control drug use, vodka disguised in water bottles. They imagine painting a word picture of the esteemed, shiny athlete with the troubled past.

Ms. Cardinal is the only one who doesn't wonder. She wipes all of her whiteboards clean. Pretends she's somewhere quiet, somewhere dark.

+

The day before the big Pep Rally, Ms. Cardinal works late. It's already past six, the light outside starting to fizzle. She sits at the table in the copier room, the printer humming to a beat that she can tap her foot to, grading last week's fractions test with a blue pen.

Today, she saw a man she didn't recognize in the hallway. He looked shorter than her, stocky, faded blue jeans baggy around the crotch. She watched him through her classroom window for five minutes, watched the way he moved, the way he stood as he chatted with students. She asked herself if he seemed slightly Roadrunner-like, before remembering that he was the custodian who empties the trashcans during second period.

The Roadrunner is more in disguise outside of his costume than he is in his costume, she thinks. She thinks she also feels this way: Ms. Cardinal the Teacher is someone different from Hannah, who she is at home.

Ms. Cardinal is halfway through her stack of tests to grade when the pen snaps. Blue ink bleeds into her palms, quickly soaks through the papers in front of her. She blinks. The printer is still spitting out papers. She waits for someone to come with a Clorox wipe, with a box of tissues to help her, but the hallways are quiet. The motion-sensor lights have actually gone off. The building is empty.

With her hands held out in front of her, Ms. Cardinal leaves the copier room and makes her way to the broom closet. She knows from her hours spent with the Roadrunner that she'll find a utility sink there and a bar of soap. All the lights in the building are automatic, and they move with her down the hallway, always delayed by just a second. She is always just a few steps ahead of the light, and in those moments of darkness, she wonders if a body lurks in the perimeters. Maybe this time when the lights come on, the Roadrunner will be there.

Ms. Cardinal pushes open the door to the broom closet with her toes and lets the light from the hallway guide her to the utility sink. As she scrubs the blue from her hand, she eyes the Roadrunner, splayed against the water heater. The Roadrunner's mesh eyes catch the light. It's easy to imagine that they're real.

She turns off the water. She leaves the door open to the hallway as she drops to her knees and finds her position next to the Roadrunner. She places her head on its shoulders, rolls up her skirt so she can throw one leg across its plush midsection. After a few moments, the lights in the hallways switch off, and the closet is all darkness and silence. She wipes her wet hands against the Roadrunner's feathered plume. She wishes it were always like this.

"Hello," she whispers. She remembers she doesn't have to be quiet and says it again, louder. "Hello."

She has a lot to say. She has spent her week imagining what she'll say to the Roadrunner. Every morning, mentally reciting a list of worries and memories to share with him. Lying here next to the Roadrunner, she is not Ms. Cardinal, she is Hannah.

"This morning," she begins. "I ran a red light. I didn't even realize I was doing it until I heard tires screech. What I mean is that I saw the red light, but I didn't know to stop. It didn't even occur to me."

The Roadrunner's face feels wet against her cheek. It startles her for a moment until she remembers it's wet from her own wet hands.

"Two days ago," she goes on, "I wanted to break into my neighbor's home while she slept. I know where she hides her key. I walked outside in my pajamas and picked up the key from under the tomato planter and went far as putting the key in the door, but all I did was unlock it. I didn't go inside. I left it unlocked, and then for the rest of the night worried about a burglar getting in and murdering her."

She pulls the Roadrunner close enough to feel its wing against her pubic bone.

"Sometimes in class, I have to whisper curse words when my back is turned, because I know that if I don't, I won't be able to stop myself from screaming them at my students."

There's a groan of pipework coming from inside the school. She sits up suddenly. It's incredible how one moment she's Hannah and the next moment she's Ms. Cardinal. She puts her legs back together. She smooths her skirt out so it rests respectfully below her knees.

It's incredible how unsafe Ms. Cardinal feels in her body.

Ms. Cardinal was always this way. Even as a teenager, she thought of her emotions as a ceramic bowl in her chest. She'd try to empty it with yoga, with long-distance running, with kissing, with dancing, but nothing would make that bowl spill.

+

"Are you going to the Pep Rally after school?" the teachers ask Ms. Cardinal in the break room the next morning.

She shrugs. She sips tea out of her Styrofoam cup. Up close, she can see that her nails are still rimmed in a thin line of blue ink.

"I hear they're only serving kale and low-fat yogurt for lunch today," Dr. Cherez says. "It's supposed to help swimmers remain buoyant."

Mr. Chuck says, “Mrs. Downton excused Martin from class today so he could go get a deep tissue massage in preparation for the race.”

Ms. Cardinal smiles with her coworkers. Ms. Cardinal isn’t going to the Pep Rally tonight, because she is tired of watching the Roadrunner dancing and jumping and shimmying from afar. She’s tired of wondering if she is catching his eye, if somehow the man in the costume senses the moments they’ve stolen together.

Tonight, she’s decided, she will meet the Roadrunner.

She sips her tea. She picks blue ink from under her nails.

+

During the pep rally, Ms. Cardinal waits in the darkened broom closet, hidden behind the water heater. She hasn’t decided if she wants the Roadrunner to see her when he arrives.

She can hear the assembly hall full of voices. The voices move like a swarm of insects, like an airplane engine, loud.

She imagines the door to the broom closet turning, imagines watching that neck unzip, that mask come off, the slow turn and reveal of a face.

But even when the stomping on the bleachers stops, and the loud ruckus of hallwaying ends, he doesn’t come. No one is coming. She falls asleep in the closet, behind the water heater, that way.

She is sore and bedheady and embarrassed when she wakes in the night. She pulls open the closet door and the motion sensor lights click on a moment later.

On the ground in front of her, in the hallway, is the Roadrunner. Face down, body splayed, not snoring. She crouches, she listens and leans over the mouthpiece feeling for heat. “Oh my god,” she says, and reaches for the zipper, reaches inside to find a pulse.

+

The thing is, there isn’t a body in there. It’s empty as it always was. It’s empty and yet it was posed like death, like it was dead, like whatever it was that was in there left.

She props the costume up against a locker. It starts to tip. She straightens it up.

Ms. Cardinal looks at it sideways, cocking her head. She unzips the neck fully. She lifts the mask over her own head. It smells like mint and dog and maybe aftershave. She swivels her head, enjoying the strangeness of a beak. Then she steps into the body of the Roadrunner, stretches her arms inside the wings, takes a moment to adjust to her new proportions.

In costume, her body disappears. She becomes the Roadrunner. She closes her eyes and feels her body evaporating like water.

She is plume, she is mesh eyes, she is soft knees.

She is three-toed feet. She is winged.

She walks into the closet, where she will feel safer, where she can explore this new body. Once in the dark of closet, she realizes how tired she still is. She yawns, her yawn hidden by beak. She falls asleep standing. It feels natural now that she’s a bird.

+

It’s hard to know how time moves in this new body. Is it the next day? Is it a week later? It must still be before the big swim meet, because when she wakes she is a body under bright, white light. Someone's voice booms over the loudspeakers NOW INTRODUCING THE ROOAAAAAAAAAADRUNNEEEEEERRRRR, and she bursts into cartwheels and sit-spins. She could never do cartwheels before, and this is not a dream. She is pumping her wings and tumbling into the cheerleaders like a bowling ball knocking down pins.

She tries to stop, but she doesn't stop. She thinks about leaving the gymnasium, running down the hallway to her old classroom, standing in the corner under the flag where she can't be seen from the door. Instead, she skips to the drumline, pounds her wing-fists against the bass drum. Instead, she inspires the teachers to start the wave.

She is doing somersaults across the three-point line when the gymnasium goes silent. No one is looking at the Roadrunner. Everyone's looking at the open gymnasium doors. She turns to look too. A crowd of boys is entering the room. They're wearing identical blue tank tops and gym shorts, and Martin Turner is leading them. Martin Turner, unsmiling and big-armed. Upon seeing him, she feels a surge of school pride, so much pride that she feels compelled to do a hand spring.

When the swim team has fully entered the gym, it's like a string has snapped inside her. She isn't tired exactly, not sad exactly. She is just done. The school screams for the swim team, and she runs away, out of the gymnasium, down the hallway to the broom closet.

She hangs herself up against the water heater like a jacket.

+

It's not a bad life, being the Roadrunner. She can listen

to the drip of the closet sink for hours. And now, she's the one they cry to. She didn't realize how many people come to the Roadrunner to talk. She likes to feel needed. She likes the press of cheeks against breastbone. She likes the sobbing sound that teachers make.

Mrs. Downton's brother is in jail for peeping on a woman in a changing room.

Ms. Philips can't have sex anymore without having an accompanying panic attack.

Dr. Cherez wakes up to a spider crawling in her ear.

Mr. Chuck spanked his toddler son for the first time and hates that it feels cathartic.

She remembers a time when this would have all been terrifying to her, but she's not scared now, and so those used-to feelings don't matter.

She hadn't realize it sucks the body out of you, this listening.

+

One day Martin Turner comes in. It's the day before the meet, and she can feel it physically in this new-body: all pep and fizzle and roar. It's hard keeping track of time when your body dissolves and reappears like an accident, like every time you're in your body you're running a red light. But she's *certain* of it.

Tonight's the big night.

Martin Turner crumples over the sink and vomits, masking the sound with running water.

He's dripping in his swim trunks. He's barefoot and fresh-shaved—all his hair, his face, his arms, his legs, his chest, which she realizes is bare. He vomits and cries a little into the sink. Every part of him is leaking.

Martin Turner says, “This fucking school.”

The Roadrunner tries to straighten up inside her body, tries to take on the posture for hearing. Maybe she succeeds, because Martin Turner glances over in her direction. His eyes are red and swollen, and the Roadrunner remembers then that he is just a kid.

Martin Turner wipes his nose and mouth with the back of his hand.

“So this is where they keep you,” he says.

He takes a step towards her. He picks her up by her wings. The Roadrunner had imagined herself heavier, is surprised her body is light enough for a boy to lift. Martin Turner looks her in the mesh eyes. “Let’s take a drive,” he says.

+

People don’t really wonder about Ms. Cardinal. They presume she called in sick, couldn’t handle all the excitement about the upcoming meet, the reporters hounding teachers on campus every day, the uptick in pep rallies. Thing is, it’s distracting, all the buzz around Martin. The star is *missing*! The day *of!* It’s six o’clock, one hour before the meet begins, and people are losing their fucking minds.

Martin Turner props up the Roadrunner in the passenger seat of his pickup. No seatbelt, so when Martin’s driving, the Roadrunner slides across the seats, folds forward at the waist, beak nestled in an empty coffee cup, legs akimbo.

It’s hard being in a body like this. It’s hard when you can’t see, can’t move the pieces you are made of.

Martin Turner has been driving for hours. He stops somewhere for French fries and the Roadrunner can smell the grease of a hamburger and feels the grime of salt when Martin rubs his hands on her like a towel. He pulls over somewhere. She realizes she's become the McGuffin in a story she didn't catch the beginning of. She is the white dress stained with red wine. She is the gun that has to go off.

Martin Turner parks and the car goes quiet. He opens his door and pulls the Roadrunner out after him, pulls her by the plume. He lets her body drop onto the ground. She feels the tar on the pavement stain her fabric skin.

They are in a parking lot at the edge of a lake. Grass. Lake. Mountains. Sky. Everything is a shade of dark blue.

"I think I'm going to put you on," Martin Turner says. He unzips her neck. He steps inside her body, what's left of it. He steps inside.

She is waiting for the lights to come on, for the auditorium full of students to roar. If enough people cheered right now, she thinks she could wrestle him out, thinks she could put herself back together again.

Martin Turner lifts the Roadrunner's head from the ground, and puts it over his head.

She's not sure what she expected. Part of her is surprised that her old body isn't still there, isn't still inside her new Roadrunner skin, shrunken up and sleeping like the smallest piece of a Russian Nesting Doll. Part of her is surprised that the moment Martin Turner put on the costume, she didn't poof out of existence.

In her skin, Martin moves toward the water. He is awkward as the Roadrunner. His arms are too big for the wings. His torso is too short. He tastes like chlorine and gum and booze.

The Roadrunner wonders what happened to the other Roadrunner. The Roadrunner before her, the one she cried to in the broom closet. Where did he, or she, go? Is he still here, still here under the mask someplace where she can't find him? Martin Turner is becoming more confident in the costume. He is running now, running toward the dark blue lake, which means she is running too. The Roadrunner remembers real running, real roads, the heavy slap of her sneakers into the pavement, the way she kept a Swiss Army Knife in her pocket, knowing any moment someone could tackle you, drag you behind a tree or into an alley—it wouldn't even have to be a shadowy place, knowing that if you are a running woman, you are easy to see as neon, you are a spotlight, a cymbal crash, open as a door with no lock.

At the edge of the lake, Martin stops.

"Who am I winning for?" he says, and his voice is absorbed into the plush of her head. His voice becomes her for a moment.

Then he takes a wide step. She doesn't feel the water, but she feels its weight. The water rushes inside of her, rushes to fill the space between her skin and Martin's. Martin keeps stepping until they are submerged up to the chest.

"Ra, Ra, ROADRUNNER!" Martin howls into the mask.

Then Martin and the Roadrunner dive. They plow their arms through the water. The Roadrunner feels what it feels like to be an Olympics-destined swimmer. She feels herself filling with water. But she doesn't notice Martin Turner filling with water too. She already lost her body, so it's hard to empathize all the pockets filling in his.

He is still kicking, still plowing, as they drift down to the bottom of the lake. It is gray down here, not blue. Algae rises around them like streamers. Martin is clutching at their neck with their wings. He thought he wanted to die, but he doesn't, not really. It was only a fantasy he thought he'd believed.

His heartbeat is so fast she can hardly stand it. She

Name M.T.

Locate on the diagram where the soul lives, if applicable.

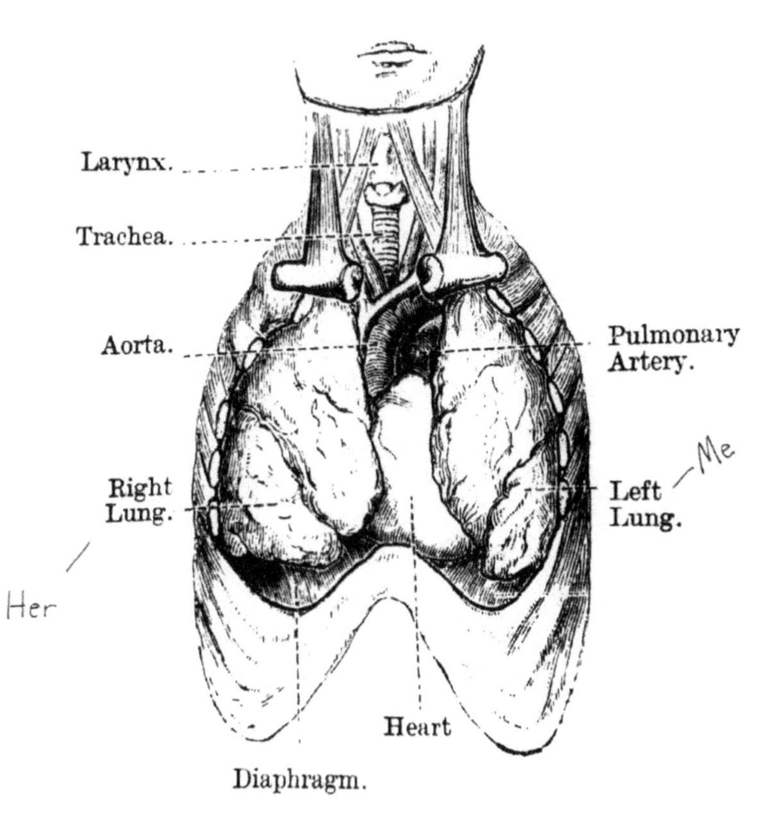

HOW TO UNVANISH A BOY

None of us expected our sons to be so good at magic. When we bought them magician kits on their sixth birthdays, we thought only of how cute it'd be to watch them fumble through decks of cards and pull fake rabbits from hats. We looked forward to pretending to be surprised when the coin vanished in the trick box. Looked forward to saying, "Wow, yes honey, that's my card," when they pulled the Queen of Diamonds instead of the Three of Clubs. We couldn't wait to feel like the good moms we knew ourselves to be. The supportive moms. The moms with endless tubes of paint and spools of yard, who learned wood-working on nights and weekends to build custom magician pushcarts.

To our surprise, we didn't have to fake astonishment when our sons pulled nickels from our ears. They made cards appear out of nowhere. Buttons vanished in their palms. "Ta-da!" they said, and we replied, "How did you do that?" In response, they held out empty hands, wiggled fingers still sticky with breakfast. They grinned smiles wide and crooked as gravel roads.

When our sons went outside to play explorer or disappeared into the living room with their iPads, we tried the tricks ourselves. We followed the directions in the manuals. We practiced sleights of hand, but the buttons always slipped between our fingers. "Ta-da!" we said, but the cards stuck together in the deck. Coins closed in our palms, but they were still there when we opened our fists.

+

It was easy to spot the other Magician Moms. At parent pick-up, they always spoke a little louder than the other moms. Their smiles disappeared when their sons' backs were turned. Teachers handed over paper bags full of confiscated items, and we could imagine what was inside: trick coins, silver rings, endless scarves.

At first, it was only once a week, but before long we were meeting every morning after we dropped our sons off at school. We canceled appointments with our personal trainers, canceled our errands to the grocery store, stood up our therapists. There was a McDonald's next to the school, so we met there. We ordered hash browns and spongy pancakes drowned in syrup. We drank coffee out of paper cups until our fingers quivered. We sat shoulder-to-shoulder in a booth at the back of the restaurant.

Tyler's mom was the first to say anything about her son being a magician. She spoke in hushed tones, as though her son might be listening from under the counter or behind the soda machine. "I don't know how to explain it," she whispered. "He made all the koi in our garden pond disappear. He won't tell us where he put them."

She looked like she might cry. We put our hands on her shoulders.

"Yesterday," another mom said, "Cameron replaced all of the eggs with mothballs. It was maddening."

"Amar has been filling his sister's make-up containers with exploding confetti."

"You think that's bad? I woke up to a closet full of toads!"

It came spilling out of us. All of the magic we'd suffered in the past weeks. We held each other's hands, nodded as we each shared the tricks we'd fallen for. Then, once we'd all spoken, we threw our soggy pancakes away and ordered Happy Meals. We filled our mouths with chicken nuggets. We ate our hamburgers with both mustard and ketchup. When we were done, we threw the toys from our Happy Meals in the trash on top of the pancakes.

We reminded each other how quickly our sons had gotten over their fighter jet phase, their mooning-their-sisters'-friends phase, their origami-throwing-star phase. This magic phase would pass, too.

"Meanwhile," one of the Moms said, "we don't want to stifle their potential."

We nodded vigorously.

We imagined a pile of magician's things burning like a Christmas tree. We imagined it going up in smoke.

+

When our sons bored of coins and decks of cards, they asked for more complicated tricks. They wanted tricks you couldn't buy at the toy store, tricks you could only get at Magic Shops. They wanted to vanish larger objects. They wanted to saw something in half. They wanted us to tie them up and throw them in the pool and time how quickly they could slip their joints from under the knots.

We told them we'd buy them new tricks if they got A's in math class, if they passed their Unit Tests, if they wrote five-paragraph essays without forgetting to indent even once. And of course, they met our demands.

"My son is too smart," one of the Moms said. "It's so hard to find a challenge he can't beat."

"Oh yes, same with my son."

"He's exactly like his father—determined and stubborn."

"GOD YES. Eric and Ethan are *identical* that way. His father used to do a little magic, too, you know. And fire-eating at a Hawaiian barbeque joint. Good Lord."

"What about Andrew?" we asked cautiously, because one of us was a single mother. "Is he like his father?"

Andrew's mom was on the inside of our booth, near the window. "Actually," she said, not meeting our eyes, "I think he takes after me." Then she stood, and we all had to get up to let her pass. "I just remembered, I have an appointment." She left her unfinished pancakes on the table.

We watched through the windows as she walked briskly to her car. She didn't drive away immediately, but we couldn't see what she was doing through the tinted windows.

We cleared our throats and pivoted a little.

"Maybe we should put a stop to this," Bryson's mother said. "Sure, it's cute now, but soon our sons will be teenagers. They'll grow facial hair. They'll want to shave their beards into soul patches."

"They'll learn how to make girls' bras unsnap without even touching them."

"They'll unlock the liquor cabinet with a silver key."

"They'll want Bengal tigers."

"They'll burn the house down."

We sipped our coffee and looked out the window. Andrew's mother was gone.

+

We agreed to buy our sons white doves, which seemed reasonable enough when we considered the alternatives: sharp-toothed saws, tiger cages, rings of fire. Our sons kept the birds in round-topped cages by their beds. They handled them often, so they got used to their always-moving hands, so they learned not to bite, not to peck. Our sons brought their doves to dinner, let their doves cling to the shower curtain rods as they showered. Our sons showed us the collapsible cages small enough to fit under one's jacket and the felt-lined pouches the doves would hide in. We found ourselves worrying for the birds. Coffee mugs cracked in our sons' hands, windows shattered, Barbie's plastic torso melted. The boys delighted in breaking what they were not allowed to break. All we could think of were the small bodies collapsing against our sons' chests, the bird bones snapping. We'd always suspected that magicians' birds had a short lifespan.

When our sons were at school, we snuck into their rooms. We stroked the doves through the bars of the cages. We were surprised to learn that doves could purr, like cats. Surprised the way they gave a little when we pressed them with a flattened palm, how they were so hollow, after all, letting out air.

+

Everything changed when our sons told us there was a school talent show. The morning after they handed us the permission slips, we breathed sighs of relief together at McDonald's. The talent show felt to us like an end point, a natural conclusion to our boys' obsession. We could feel it with certainty, as if the future were streaming in front of us—after the curtain rose, and the boys bowed, and we all went home. We could feel ourselves folding up the capes and flattening the trick magicians' hats. We could sense the space we would make for it in the back of the closet, and how the costumes would live there, under winter sweaters, for the rest of their lives.

We started to prepare. We emailed each other coupons and carpooled to Michaels to stock up on glitter. We had our husbands build magician carts and met up in the afternoons to decorate them together. Also, we started keeping secrets. One afternoon Joni let it slip that Devon would be incorporating a comedy routine, and as we murmured approvingly, we noticed something check off in one another's eyes: *That's a good idea,* and soon after, *My son is actually funnier than hers.* A few days later, Trish had patterns to alter a bridesmaid's dress into something more magician's-assistant-like, and suddenly we all were making patterns. It only made sense to become more secretive.

We noticed, with some relief, that Andrew's Mom was always running late, always short on carpenter's glue, always maneuvering her second-hand magician's cart awkwardly before letting it clatter out of her hatchback. It gave us something that tied us together. Some of us were serious competitors, and some of us were, well.

We held our phones close to our chests and smiled sharply at one another.

Our sons were impressive, yes, but maybe talent wasn't enough.

Over the next few days, we bought our sons black silk capes, red roses. Promised to let ourselves be sawed in half. Reconsidered tricks involving fire. Smiled tight smiles at each other.

We started to get the feeling that each of us was investigating each other on the sly. That each of us had an arsenal of secrets against the other. That it wasn't safe to be casual friends. That none of us were really to be trusted.

We stopped seeing one another at the McDonald's so much.

One by one, we dropped off the group-text chains.

Started throwing shade in the parking lot.

"Junior's got a real knack for magic," said one of us through the car window at parent pick-up.

One of us bought security cameras for the house, padlocks for the closets.

Another unfriended the rest of us on Facebook.

Because there was always this other, murkier part of us that wanted our son to be The Best. To levitate, to set ablaze, to emerge unscathed from a tiger's mouth.

In this way, we disintegrated. No longer a cohesive unit. Just a legion of I's.

II.

I had my own secrets I'd been keeping. My son Andrew could disappear.

It started a couple weeks after the magician obsession began. Sometimes he turned translucent during dinner when I asked him to finish his meat. This wasn't card-trick magic. I reached for him one time as he was turning, and my hand passed through his arm, touching the back of the chair behind him. He reappeared in the living room, perched on the arm of the couch, laughing.

He disappeared in the frozen foods aisle of the grocery store. He disappeared at bed time.

"Andrew," I told him, "you are not disappearing anymore, do you understand me?"

At this, he vanished his face, leaving his body and neck but no eyes for mine to sink into.

"I mean it, young man," I told the space where his face belonged, "or there will be no more magic. We will be dropping out of the talent show if this behavior continues."

I was the only single Magician Mom. The only one who

couldn't pick up her son at 3:30, who had to sign him up for the After-School Program and pick him up two hours after school ended. I thought about asking the other Moms for advice, but I knew what they'd say behind my back:

"If she was home more, maybe he'd listen to her and she wouldn't have this problem in the first place."

"He needs a traditional family. Two parents. He'll run away from home at the first chance he gets."

The worst part was, I wondered if they were right.

I thought back to a year ago when I'd wake up to Andrew burrowed next to me in bed, fleeing a nightmare. A year ago, he'd sprint through the house, naked like a wild animal, and whisper his dreams to me over breakfast. Now, he hid from me. Behind doors, behind magic. Now, his body and his thoughts were a mystery to me.

A year ago, Andrew had two parents. And sure, he *still* had two parents, but one of them lived far away now. Avery Skyped in once a week, always on Sunday. She'd ask Andrew to show her his magic tricks and *oohed* and *aahed* when she was supposed to. She clapped awkwardly over Skype. Sometimes her face disintegrated into pixels when the bandwidth was lousy, sometimes her cat—the one she got when she moved to Singapore—shoved its way into the frame, purring so loud you could hear it through the computer speakers. But Andrew never showed her his real tricks. I didn't know whether I should feel flattered or hurt that he only vanished in front of me.

+

The day before the talent show, Andrew disappeared all night. I spent the hours baking his favorite desserts, trying to lure him out of wherever he went when he vanished. I called the school in the morning, saying he had the flu. I didn't go in to work. I waited, standing in the kitchenette, making blueberry pancakes, wondering if, by the time I stacked them thirty high, he'd be back. I thought about calling Avery. Avery could make pancakes shaped like Mickey Mouse, I remembered. But she wouldn't believe me. She would think I lost him, when really he had lost me. How could I explain that our boy was a mystery to me now?

When Andrew finally did reappear—floating on the kitchen ceiling, legs crossed in lotus pose—I wondered how I was supposed to mother someone who didn't even obey the laws of gravity.

"We're going to school now," I said, not caring that I would be bringing him in two hours late. I let him eat the pancakes in the car. I didn't care about the crumbs.

At school, a few of the other Magician Moms were dropping off their sons late, too. They had dark circles under their eyes. Mary stopped me outside the front office, babbling about waking up to the garage completely empty—both cars, the power tools, the washer *and* dryer full of clothes. Her husband tried to phone the police. Her boy had grabbed his iPhone and twisted his wrist, returning the device as a dove.

Ethan's mom came in with bandages around her torso. Her hair was singed. I remembered when all of us had joked about sawing-in-half tricks. I remember the covetous way her hands wrapped around a coffee cup, how whole she seemed then, how different she looked now.

"Talent show's tonight," one of them said absently.

"Should be great," one of them responded. "Best of luck, really."

They meandered away, together. They meandered together, away.

+

I'd already taken the day off, so I drove home instead of to work. I sat at the kitchen table and drank the lukewarm coffee I'd made earlier that morning. The next time my son disappeared, I didn't want to be powerless. A few weeks ago, I'd bought a spell book on eBay, *A Mother's Conjuring: 200 Spells for the Family and Household.* I'd never really tried them in earnest. I had bought the book as a prop to show Andrew I was interested in his hobbies.

I retrieved the book from the living room and put my feet up on the coffee table. I flipped through the index.

Tidiness.

Obedience.

Curfew.

Reconciliation.

There was nothing under 'reappear.' But there was an entry on magicians.

Magicians are a mother's worst nightmare. If one is living with a magician, one must work against his strengths: fanfare, silk, black smoke, mirrors. However, the most important asset of a magician is audience. Without an audience, the magician has no purpose. Disimbue the magic of your household by withholding attention. Remove the reflective surfaces from your home. Let in as much unfiltered light as possible. Confiscate (or eliminate) his materials. Witches will use a fire and cast a sealing spell to contain any malignant properties that remain. Remember: as a mother, you are imbued with certain powers.

I wondered what those powers were. If mine were

stronger than Avery's. If there was a mothering power between us that had been stretched too far, thinned somehow. Frayed, now that she was gone.

+

Flipping around in the book a bit, I found a spell for conjuring. It seemed close enough. I wanted to see if I could make Andrew appear now, disappear him out of his desk chair at school and reappear him here.

I said the magic words. Squeezed my eyelids tight.

But Andrew did not appear.

I wandered up to his room, looking for powders or emblems that might make the spell stronger. What I found were the doves, Macy and Gerald, preening their feathers. I stuck my hand in their cage and squeezed my fingers around them, felt their little jackhammer hearts against my palms. They didn't struggle. I stuck them in my sweater pockets.

I saw Andrew's magic box, shut and locked and spray-painted gold. A pack of matches he'd been using to sear holes through quarters. *Witches use a fire*, I thought, and pocketed those too. I wrapped my arms around the magic box like I was hugging it. It was heavy but I managed to carry it down the stairs, out the backdoor, and into the yard.

The doves cooed inside my sweater. I wondered if they could sense the outside, if they could hear distant birds chirping in distant trees.

I made a tiny flame with a match and held it to the grass next to the box until I could smell it burning.

I could feel small talons through the fabric. I pulled the doves from my pockets and opened my palms. They flapped to a nearby tree branch and perched, blinking down at me.

The box began to crackle.

While it did, a tiny raincloud appeared overhead, which I could only presume to be my son. I focused very hard on not looking up, not losing composure when my son turned the sky to sleet, then sharp pellets of hail. I could hear amassing storm clouds, and when lightning hit the ground a few feet away from me, I nearly broke.

But I would not break.

The magic box burned. Decks of cards curled, the silk cape shimmered, his top hat caved in on its burning self. Everything a molten lump.

The more it burned the more my son surrounded me. And maybe that was my motivation, after all. Maybe the thought of another disappearance in my life was too much to bear. Avery over the ocean. Andrew up in the air.

My face smudged with ashes. My legs warmed from the fire. I marched back to the house against the downpour, without looking up, reciting a spell in my head like a prayer. I did not pay my blowing, raining son any mind. I wanted him to know the feeling I was so accustomed to feeling. I was the transparent one now.

III.

We noticed right away that Andrew and his mom weren't at the talent show. We thought to ourselves, "So unreliable." We thought, "It's too bad for Andrew, really."

We sat in the front row of foldable chairs set up in the gym. We held up signs splattered in glitter. We gave thumbs-ups to our sons, who stood in line beside the wood-box stage.

Ethan was first. He dropped his cups trying to make a ball disappear. We clapped politely and secretly fist pumped. Then Tyler's caged doves squirmed against his breast pocket, revealing the trick. The spotlight was so bright on Cameron you could see the hidden container inside his top hat.

Onstage, our sons were... nothing. How did they go from boys who could make entire rooms disappear to boys who couldn't do simple parlor tricks? We felt ourselves burning, wondering if we'd imagined the whole thing, why it wasn't working now, in public.

Magicians are nesting dolls, we realized. They are boys equipped with trapdoors. One of our sons' loose rabbits hurried offstage and was caught by the ballerina who played violin. She was later crowned the talent show winner. It was all so natural to her, as it was natural the way our sons shed their capes like a chrysalis.

We threw away our programs on the way out the door. We threw away our signs. Our sequins. Our ideas, of being the best.

IV.

The house was so empty, without the cooing of doves. Without Andrew. Without Avery.

Thinking a name is the same as conjuring, the spell book advised. I tried to think 'her' instead. I tried to think 'the boy.'

The boy, I thought. Maybe I should say 'the rain.' Maybe 'the permafrost,' unseasonable and clinging to the windowpanes.

I staggered into the kitchen, dripping wet. Set the matchbook on the countertop. Peeled my sweater off. Wrung it out into an empty bowl.

Wondered what it would be like at this moment if there was another mother here, and not just me.

Upstairs, I heard a sound like a book dropping, and then footsteps. The creak of a mattress. Soon, I'd go up to my son. I'd go to him, not sure if anything would really change for me, not sure if these disappearances were the first in a long line of distances we'd experience. I'd hold him to my chest anyway. I'd hold my son against the hard of my ribs and push the hairs back from his forehead. Soon. But for now, I'm imbued with certain powers. The book said I am imbued. That I am powerful in ways I don't even know yet. I want him to feel my absence for a moment. I want his ears aching for the sounds of my feet on the stairs.

POSTCARD

PLACE
STAMP
HERE

Remember ~~when you got~~
your head got stuck
in the banister? And
when you found a broken bird
+ fed it worms you
mashed yourself?
~~And it never flew?~~
I loved that – seeing
you that way

SPY GIRL

Spy Girl currently has three cases. The Case of the Missing 6. The Case of Bird-Stuck-In-The-Gymnasium. The Case of Lost-And-Found-Scarf. She expects that she will solve them all by Monday, but by then she might have new ones.

Spy Girl goes to Spy School after regular school. Spy School has a diverse student body. At seven years old, Spy Girl is the youngest in her class, but that doesn't mean she doesn't have a rich social life. At Spy School, Spies start intermural basketball teams and disco bands. Practice starts at two AM and goes until the sun rises. Everyone wants Spy Girl to be their lead singer, their offensive player, their co-Spy.

+

I am not supposed to have favorites. Spy Girl isn't as smart as Android Boy, not as nice as the Unicorn Twins, not as funny as Astronaut Girl. But Spy Girl appreciates a secret. Of all my students, she's the only one who doesn't tattle when Booger Boy eats his boogers. She has the air of a child who already understands that the world is full of mostly-not-good people. She keeps her hair short and braided. She wears sneakers and high socks so her shins won't be scratched when she crawls through an air vent or scales a brick wall.

One day when I find a tissue box on my laptop, I know it's from her. The tissues have been removed, and the box contains bird feathers, a large stone, a toothpick, a deformed charm abandoned from some bracelet. When I ask her what it means, she says she doesn't know. She tells me what I tell her during art class when we've run out of paper, or when the pencil sharpener jams: Problem Solve. So now I watch her out the windows during recess. How she moves carefully over the surface of things. How she stoops, examines, picks up.

+

I'm a young teacher. Guessing my age is one of my students' favorite pastimes. They leave notes on my laptop when I'm away in the bathroom. *Miss Deal, are you twenty-seven? Twenty-eight? Twenty-nine? Miss Deal, are you thirty-two? Miss Deal, are you older than a mature alligator? Miss Deal, are you as old as Sacajawea when she left with Lewis and Clark or younger?*

I press pastels to their fingertips, show them elementary watercolor technique, show them how to make a mobile, show them how to fold paper into cranes.

I am still struggling with what it means to be a Teacher. I experiment with wearing knee-length dresses patterned with grinning 2-point pencils and frolicking dinosaurs. I experiment with wearing earrings shaped like radishes, like globes. I experiment with wearing short dresses with no leggings. I experiment with wearing leggings with no pants. I haven't decided if I want to be Nice Teacher or Edgy Teacher or Fantasy Teacher or Bra-Straps-Are-Always-Showing-But-Not-In-A-Sexy-Way Teacher.

I spend my weekends chewing down my fingernails

instead of painting like I said I would, thinking, How can I be expected to believe that everyone deserves to be happy because they are human? Thinking, If I were the Unicorns Twins' mother would I put bows on their horns or grow their bangs out to cover them up?

When I find a shoebox on my porch that is full of petals, I almost throw it into the air to see if I am Flower Child Teacher, but I am glad I don't because when the petals push aside I see a flattened bird at the bottom. It looks like it might have been a finch, but I only ever pretend to know birds' names. When I see Spy Girl on the playground the following day, she is sprawled out on her back, a fresh kill in a game. Why are children always killing each other in games? Why is there always lava, earthquakes, alligators? I watch Airplane Boy shake the wooden bridge while the children run across it screaming. I watch Airplane Boy get into his tiny him-sized plane at the end of the school day and take off into the air, as though it were nothing.

+

Sometimes I think of Spy Girl when I go grocery shopping. I imagine her hiding in the pyramid of limes, nose and cheeks painted yellow-green. When I reach for a carton of eggs, I imagine her on the other side of the shelves, eyelashes thick in the frosty shadows. When I go clothes shopping at the mall, I separate the hangers, the curtains of fabric, half expecting Spy Girl to be crouched at their center.

Maybe that's why when I bump into a man in the frozen food section, I'm not surprised to see Spy Girl watching me from behind the shelf of chocolate sauce at the end of the aisle. The man makes me laugh, and I touch my hand to his arm as though I'm landing a plane. Spy Girl comes up to us and pokes her head around his body.

"This is Lori," he says to me, and I do the right thing just then: I act as though I have never met her.

"Hi there, Lori. I'm Amanda." I'm using a code name. I've decided I'm a spy-girl too. Dave – that's his name – asks me what I do. I tell him I'm a nurse. I tell him it's been a long day drawing blood. I tell him a woman came in at three with a Lego-man stuck up her nose. Spy Girl doesn't bat an eye. I don't bat an eye. I'm Amanda, the blood-drawing, Lego-removing nurse. And when he asks me out to dinner in the checkout line, I line up my lemons in rows and say, yes, of course, I'd like that.

+

In art class we are working with plaster, and I bring in a dummy's head to demonstrate how to cast a face.

"First you prepare your work area," I say, but what I mean is: you are going to make a mess.

We draw yards of protective plastic across the surfaces of tables, we spread newspaper on the floor, we don our smocks, we tie our hair back, all of us, and we get out the materials – the stuff dentists use to cast teeth.

We don't finish, of course, before the 50 minutes is used up – we've barely covered anything – only the curve of the nose, only one cheek. But Spy Girl wants to stay in from recess to start over. I tell her she can. I tell her anyone can change their face.

+

I live as though Spy Girl is always watching. I buy a coat with a hood just so I can duck into it. I wear concealer, conceal myself in long sleeves, dark colors, even at night. I walk with the wind to my back. When I am not a teacher I am incognito, pouring through racks of discount scrubs at Savers, wrapping gauze over imaginary wounds, lining my life with lies. Dave is coming over, and I'm boning up on anecdotes. I wonder what a nurse drinks, what she watches on TV. I set two electric candles on the table. I lavish stemmed grapes onto a plate. I leave kicked-off slippers near the sofa. What do nurses listen to? How do nurses wait? I decide to crack the window, let the night air push in. When I push Dave down on the bed, do I need to be medical, procedural? Do I ask him about STIs? A nurse probably would. Although, maybe I'm the nurse who wouldn't. Maybe I'm the reckless sort of woman who loves the blood and bone more than sewing it up. Maybe I'm always trying to get to the insides of things. Maybe that's what I'll say, when he asks me. When he says, I didn't expect you to be this way, I can say, Neither did I.

+

Spy Girl stays in from recess, even though she's already finished her plaster cast. She stays in to tell me that she is not really a Spy Girl. She made up the night school, the basketball teams. She made up the Case of the Missing 6, so she could also make up the solution. She left me boxes of stuff she found on the playground, so I would make it real with her. She tells me this expecting that I already know, but I don't want to believe it. I tell her, Number 1 wants a complete report by sundown, no excuses.

She stands on one side of my desk, and I stand on the other. She sighs and shakes her head like I'm the one who doesn't understand. Spy Girl rolls her socks down her shins and tucks them into her shoes. When she leaves, I pull one of her assignments out from my "Hand Back" pile. I leave a cryptic note in disappearing red ink.

My friend, who is a teacher at a different school, says that she also has a Spy Girl. Her Spy Girl has a Spy Hideout in the janitor's closet, and last month solved the Case of the Missing Fog Machine. She saved their theater department almost two-thousand dollars.

I become defensive of my Spy Girl. I say that my Spy Girl is humble, keeps her cases small. She helps the individual, not the corporation.

My friend tells me that sounds just fine, that everyone has their own skillset, but I can tell she's judging my Spy Girl. I watch Spy Girl in the hallways, hoping she's planning something big. But she's stopped carrying around her notebook with her. She's started growing out her hair.

I try, in my ways, to reach out to her. I track in muddy footprints. I leave a file folder labeled TOP SECRET on the floor. Astronaut girl picks it up and hands it to me. Astronaut girl isn't lying when she says she didn't look inside. She fastens on her helmet before recess, smooths her silver suit.

+

Dave sees me on parent-teacher night. I am holding the microphone in one hand and a crayon drawing of Abraham Lincoln in the other. I have *Ms. Deal* in large letters on the nametag pinned to my blouse. I am wearing the skirt I wore to the supermarket when he met me, and I met me, the alternate-me, the Amanda. I don't even notice him until the lights go up and splash across his cheekbones. Dave stands with a pamphlet over his heart. I spot Spy Girl poking up from in the shadows beneath the trashcan lid, narrowing her eyes at me. So she hasn't stopped being a Spy Girl, I think.

When Dave approaches, I thrust my hand out at him. I am good at undercover now. I am good at making my hand feel like a stranger's hand. Amanda? he says. And I tap my nametag and furrow my eyebrows. And I say, Oh - with a smile - that's my sister. I have a mole on my stomach, and that's how you can tell. It's so weird, being twins.

I know he's supposed to meet me, the Amanda-me, later, in a theatre, but I make no rush to leave the school. I make sure he leaves before I do. Spy Girl must be with him. I lift the trashcan lid, shake out the black bag, just to be sure. I tuck my hair behind my ears and fold my arms and leave.

It's hard for me, being a Spy Girl. At home I shower and strip off all my clothes. I can't smell like a school. I need to smell like a hospital. I make a small incision across my ankle, use cottonballs and peroxide, bandage the hell out of myself. I splash my neck with peroxide and rub hand sanitizer over my hands. I pull my hair back into a ponytail, go outside and smoke. I've never seriously smoked, but it seems like what Amanda would do. Smoke between shifts, to keep her hands steady. I hope menthols are ok. I hope using my paring knife for an incision is ok. I wince when I bend my ankle. I tap the ashes off the porch. Inside I color the spaces under my eyes as if I just woke up, and I'm blowing off the night shift.

+

For days I don't see Spy Girl. Her chair is empty, her cubby neat. It is like a ghost has moved in where she used to be. No one notices the mysterious way the Unicorn Twins have sharpened their horns, how Booger Boy sneaks a calculator out of his cargo shorts and punches numbers but no one can figure out what he's calculating. The lights flicker when it's lunchtime, and no one seems curious. No one notices when Manny passes a note to Almanzo, who passes a note to Nathan, who passes a note to August. No one notices that I've taped my toes together inside my shoes, that I'm experimenting with breaking and setting tiny bones, that my pinky is next.

+

I am a popular teacher. The children shout my name when they see me in the hallway. They are always hugging. Walking through the hallway during class change is like walking through a field of nettles. Small hands clinging. They touch the fringe of my scarf. They grab my pinky, now broken and set on a tiny splint. They reach for the pleats in my skirt. I'm not supposed to hug back. I have to be careful with the physical space. But I let them hug me, while resting a hand safely on the edge of their shoulder. They care more about hugging than being hugged.

Not all of them are like this. Some of them aren't babies anymore. Some of them have already grown tall, aware of their size and space. They don't hug. They don't reach for your hand.

When Spy Girl returns, she's like this. It's like she's taller now, it's like she's adopted a new identity, a quiet daytime persona. She joins the actual basketball team. She brings star-shaped suckers for a birthday treat. She plays clap-games with girls who don't have horns, who don't wear space suits. She calls herself Amanda, even though she isn't.

+

Dave invites me to his place for a movie, and I decide to

show up in my newest pair of scrubs. Purple, V-necked, with a tiny cactus print. I think about splashing some dyed corn syrup on the pants and calling it blood, but worry he'd think I'm a clumsy nurse, the kind who'd miss her patient's vein or forget to dab a puncture wound with a cotton ball before applying the bandage.

Dave lives in a first-floor duplex close to the school. He answers the door after my first knock, and I am breathless, all Sorry-I-Just-Got-Off-Work-Sorry-I'm-A-Mess. He says I'm exquisite, pulls me inside. The living room is classic bachelor pad, all Ikea furniture, all sharp square edges and black particle board, scent of Clorox, freshly sprayed, in the air.

"Where's Lori?" I ask, and he says she's with her mother.

I want this to mean something. I want this to be a clue. While he pulls my scrubs over my head, off my hips, I look for tiny girl shoes kicked under the loveseat, trails of crumbs on the coffee table, dog-eared magazines.

"So weird you have a twin. I would've believed she was you," he says, rubbing a thumb along the ridges left on my hip by the elastic waist band. He's speaking into my neck. "Lori talks about her all the time. Your sister's well-liked."

Who's he more attracted to, I wonder, Sexy-Nurse or Sexy-Teacher? I think about picking him up as Teacher-Me, seducing him in my classroom under the plaster planet mobiles, starting a love triangle where two corners are myself.

We roll around on his futon-couch for a while, and when Dave finally puts on a movie, he falls asleep almost immediately, head tilted back against the cushions.

Something about the steadiness of his breathing, the apartment so quiet I can hear the cubes in the freezer when the ice machine turns over, makes me hyper-awake, alert. I inhale and ease myself slowly off the couch cushions. I'm barefoot, pad silent on the carpet. I become a Spy Girl again. A Spy Girl in wrinkled nurse disguise.

Dave's duplex has only four rooms, and so I test doorknobs, peer into the dark spaces, wipe my fingerprints off the knobs with the sleeve of my scrubs. I find a room with a twin bed piled with stuffed animals and go inside. Shut the door. I use my cellphone to light up the corners blue. I'm depressed by how bare the walls are, how the animals on her bed are the animals you'd expect for a girl: bears, horses, frogs.

I want to leave Lori something. A stethoscope or an earring hook or a tooth with its root still intact. I want her to know that things aren't as they appear, there are people with secrets, people with broken toes hidden inside shoes. I want to save her from being Lori. Save her from being a girl with a girl's name.

Outside, in the hallway, the floor squeaks. Instinctually I drop, ease my body under the bed. I press my bare feet against the wall. Draw myself back and become tiny under the box-springs. Lori's door opens, and there are Dave's feet, sock-clad in the doorway.

I haven't had time to decide who I am yet, I think. I think, Please don't come closer.

Beside me, I feel breathing.

It's soundless but I feel it. And it's soundless, but it's her.

Clue 1: The SECRET NUMBER is NOT the number of times you thought about slipping a death cap into Space Heater Boy's tuna salad.

Clue 2: The SECRET NUMBER is less or equal to how many crow feathers you found underneath the tire swing.

Clue 3: The SECRET NUMBER is (x) more than the number of times you were not called on, even though you had your hand up.

The Secret Number is ______________________ .

THE END OF AMBER

When a star is broken, it makes a lip-smack sound. When a star is broken, it turns to glass that can prick your fingers and gives you a rash that will glow bright white at night. This is all we know about the stars at first. Our janitor drops them one day, and we crouch low to the ground in the school hallways before reaching out and, gingerly, picking them up. We've never seen anything like them before.

The stars are small as acorns. They're white like salt crystals and very, very pretty in a way that we can't really compare to anything else. We throw them against the playground sidewalk and hear them pop like firecrackers. We trade them at lunch and during study hall. One star in exchange for the answers to the circulatory system quiz. Three stars for breaking into the Dean's office and getting Kelly's cellphone back. We don't know the stars' value yet, so we trade them for petty things.

+

The closer the stars are to our bodies, the more we notice ourselves changing.

We're twelve and see everything. We see when Kelly swallows a star on a dare and says, "They make you feel like a rock whipping along the asteroid belt."

We see how Gabriel turns stars into earrings for his many girlfriends, wrapping them in wire and hanging them on hoops of sterling silver. And afterwards, we see how the girls point towards him almost magnetically, zeroed in on his locker in passing period, carving his name in desks and bathroom stalls. We see how when the stars in the girls' hoops start to fade, the glow dimming down to black, the light behind their eyes does too. They move on to other boys, and Gabriel crafts more earrings.

Those of us who've held a star feel something itching in us when we don't have them. We feel like we're starving to death. We feel our hearts turn to hummingbirds when we sense a hint of sharpness, a hint of glow. Some of us try to find stars on our own—at the quarry where sometimes you'll come across a fossil, in the health food store on the corner that sells weird bundles of herbs and bottled oils. But we only ever find stars around the janitor.

We start to follow him like bloodhounds.

Stake out his supply closet.

Break into his car, search the glove compartment, under the rugs, in the trunk, feel victorious after each star we find.

We get busted, some of us, caught and sent to detention, and when they confiscate our stars we pretend they're minerals, something for science class, and while we're still in trouble, we're in 'trouble' the way the weirdos are: too passionate about science class, they guess. Too into rocks.

We steal our stars back the first chance we get and hold them so close to our hearts our bodies pulsate.

Kelly, Amber, Gabriel, and me – we've been close all our lives.

But with the stars, we're closer than ever before.

+

Amber's whole family is really into hunting.

What I mean is: she has access to a lot of guns.

It's me and Kelly and Gabriel and one of his many girlfriends—I wanna say Liz?—her stars still glowing and swinging from her ears, and Amber of course, with this haircut and winged mascara that makes her look sixteen even though she's like the rest of us: scrawny and stupid and twelve.

We hang out in the kitchen eating spicy Cheetos while her dad drinks beer in front of the TV. She tells us it takes like six beers, and then he's out. Gabriel gets bored and heads towards the woods behind Amber's house, and he takes Liz, his hand on her butt.

"Gross," I say, to see what Amber will say.

But she's rummaging in the fridge for more soda.

We're all into Amber, everyone at school, but me the most. Me: patient and near. Me: a friend, and so, an almost boyfriend. I see what the stars can do to girls. I see Liz's bra straps showing and Gabriel plucking them affectionately in the hallway.

I have no idea what love is like and so I am learning from what I see.

What I see is Amber pulling the stars she's been saving out of her pockets.

I have some I've been saving too.

"I bet it's better than a bullet," Amber says, licking the cheese dust off her fingers. "I bet it goes, like, straight through a tree."

"I'm gonna film it," says Kelly. "YouTube. Instagram. We're gonna be famous."

"For shooting a gun?" I say.

"For shooting a *star*," she gushes. "Oh my god, guys. Shooting STARS. It's perfect."

After her dad has like six beers, Amber eases her way

under her parents' bed and pulls out her father's hunting rifle. I wipe my cheese dust on my jeans and finger the star in my pocket. I've held onto it so long it's smooth as sea glass. We creep out the door and close it by hand so the screen door won't slap. Then Amber and Kelly and me head out to the forest at last.

+

It's late afternoon. The sky is doing that dusky thing, orangey-red, that makes the forest look haunted. I think about curfew, how my mother said 9 o'clock with such sharp finality. We crunch across the broken sticks and dead leaves and get so far into the woods we can't see Amber's house.

Gabriel and Liz are mostly kissing each other against a tree, but Amber's the boss, and when Amber says, "Get your tongue out of her throat," Gabriel listens like a well-trained dog.

We gather around her.

She loads a star into the gun, pulls back on something—the safety?—and aims straight ahead at a pine tree.

I'm standing so close I think I can feel her heartbeat.

When the gun goes off—my God. It's *instantaneous*. A blasting burst of light, and the whole tree catches fire, its needles hot red.

"Holy shit!" cries Kelly.

The flames make a roaring sound. Amber stumbles backwards from the recoil. I catch her in my arms and for a few seconds I'm holding her. But it's faster than you'd think, how the brush around us catches, and soon Amber has gotten back to her feet.

"Shit, shit, shit, this was so stupid," Amber's saying, clinging to me. It's a hissing, hungry sound around us, the fire enormous, the way we can feel the flames through our shoes.

I say, "RUN," and suddenly I'm the boss, and we grab onto one another and it's five of us in a line running through flames, and somehow we're not burning, and somehow, when we break through the forest, all of us are alive.

+

It's all anyone talks about at school for a while. In science class, we hound our teachers. How can there be a fire without a cause, why doesn't it burn itself out, why can't the fire department extinguish it? It's embarrassing for our teachers. They try to say: scientists are always asking questions, and these are great questions! Luckily no one can trace the outbreak of the forest fire back to us, and that thing *burns* for days. The fire department doesn't understand. It's not like normal fire, they keep saying, inadequately, on TV. We laugh at them on our lunch breaks. Sling mustard-covered bologna onto the cafeteria floor where the janitor mops it up.

+

After the forest fire, Amber is in love with me. Gabriel seems very impressed, and Kelly annoyed, and Liz doesn't care, but I care, and I also feel shitty. A little bit guilty. Because I have a secret. When she fell into my arms in the forest, I placed a star in her ear. She didn't even notice it. Like I've said, I'd worn the star down smooth. It was small. It glowed faintly through her hair, hard to notice it unless you knew what to look for. Amber lays her head on my shoulders now. Now, she looks at me like I am the sun and moon. In brief moments when we find ourselves alone, she wraps her arms around me so tight we feel like one person, and she brushes her lips against my neck, and I am more electric than I've ever been.

We sneak out to her woods sometimes, and she presses me into a tree and kisses me so hard my heart rockets.

And when the glow in her star starts to fade, I replace it with another. And another.

I could marry this woman, I think.

And I picture the forest on fire.

+

The problem is, by mid-winter there are almost no more stars left. You can tell because the sky is slowly getting blacker, and those of us taking astronomy are noticing how impossible it is to read the sky. There's still some up there, but, like, no way to get our hands on them. It's February, and the ankles of our boots are packed with snow and our knuckles are chapped raw. Some guys on the baseball team sell pieces of quartz, trying to pass them off as the real thing. A girl ends up in the hospital with a rock stuck in her colon.

I don't have any more stars, and I know this might be the end of Amber.

On my own, I start watching the janitor more closely.

Maybe our janitor has gotten wiser, maybe he's started carrying his stars around in plastic baggies that he keeps hidden in his shirt. I trail him through the hallways when I'm supposed to be at lunch. I invent stomach aches to send me to the nurse, and instead spy on him washing the second-floor windows.

Amber turns to me in math class and mouths the words, "I love you."

I think: I can't lose this.

I'm asking myself desperately: where does the janitor keep his stars? Where does he get them? What does he use them for?

When I walk by him, I'm almost taller than him now. I try to brush by him to feel for anything lumpy or star-shaped. He's gruffer than I remembered, says, "Hey. Watch it." After school I sometimes see him head into CVS for a six-pack, throw one back in the cab of his truck before heading out. I see him get to school early to scrape ice off of the classroom windows. I see him smoking outside sometimes, and I pick up the discarded butts, searching for a glow, a faint sharpness, that feeling one gets when close to stars.

One morning, I get to school early. I tell my mom I feel like walking, and bundle up and wear my snowboots, and she's okay with it. She's been nicer to me since I got a girlfriend.

It takes like 30 minutes, but it gives me time to think.

I think about her, of course.

I've started thinking of her as 'her' because it's easier, because I'm going to lose her, because I'm twelve and an idiot and what I've learned about love is that it's like a fire: it needs kindling and attention, it needs to be stoked, it needs to breathe.

And when I get close to the school, I see him. Our janitor. And he isn't scraping ice. He's standing in his truck bed, his breath hanging in front of his face, and I hide behind the hedgerows to watch.

And I see him with a lasso.

And I see him throw it upwards into the sky and loop it around a star, and yank so hard his body quivers, and pull it in. I can tell it's heavy.

He does this like ten times.

Ten tiny stars.

I do the math in my head: if a star lasts, like, 2 months, and there are 10 stars there... My throat burns. I think of Amber. I think of growing old together. What does growing old together look like? Slowly holding hands while they wrinkle? Learning how to cook, how to have sex? Picking out a cat together and naming him a kind of human name, like Vincent or Ernie?

A car pulls into the parking lot: sleek and black, with tinted windows. The janitor jumps down from the truck bed, knocks on the driver's window, waits for it to roll down a crack. He's talking to the driver for a second, then hands over the stars. A white envelope is passed back. The janitor takes it, stuffs it in the back of his pants.

Oh, I think. Shit.

The black sedan glides out of the parking lot and around the corner. The janitor watches it, pulls out a cigarette and smokes it down to the nub. Then heads back to his truck, sits in the cab, turns it on. He doesn't drive. So...what the hell is he doing? I kind of crabwalk my way closer through the snow, careful to be as quiet as possible.

And when I look in the cab, I see he has one still. A single, tiny star. My heart leaps. Yes! There's still a chance, I think.

He's holding it and it glows. He's holding it, and he's holding it, and he's holding it, and he's holding it. And the look in his eyes is so pure and, like, naked almost. I feel like I'm intruding on something. I crouch low and shake my head to clear it. I think about how I'll wait for just the right moment. I'll watch.

I'm practiced in the art of patience.

I know how to do what's next.

Sketch the Sky

What constellations can you see at night?

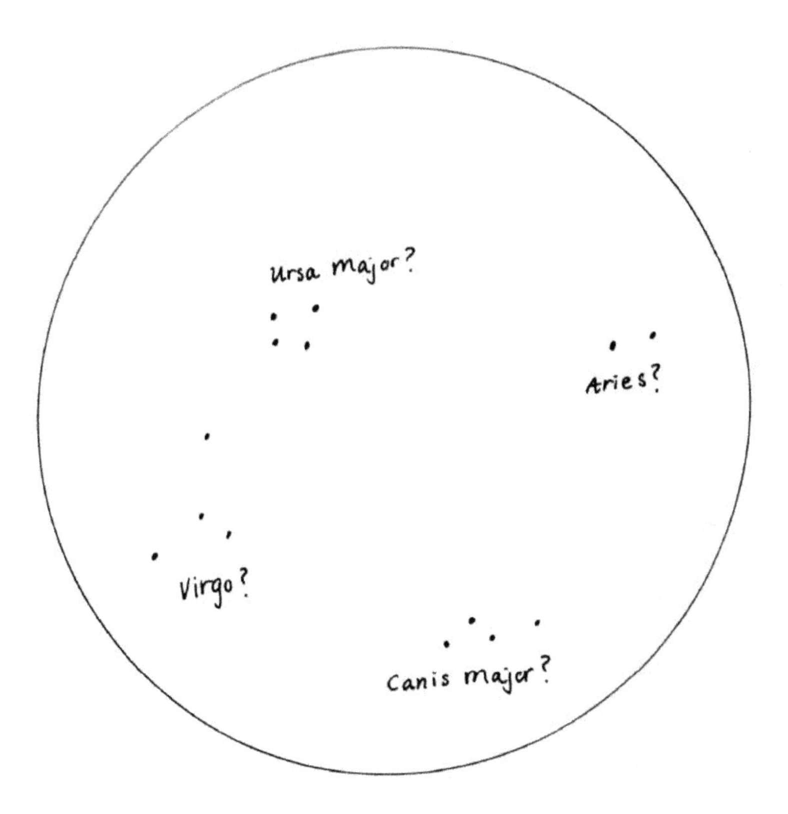

ANYTHING CAN BE A WEAPON

When the zombies overtook the Lakeshore School District, the Dads were the first to go. They were crossword Dads. Whiskery and near-sighted. They were dads with novelty bowties. Some say the zombies took the Dads first because they were the strongest, because the zombies were building an army and needed strong soldiers. But we know the truth. The Dads were the first to go because they were easy targets. When they got cornered in drug store parking lots, in movie theater bathrooms, in art galleries held in warehouses, we know it's because they never learned to fear corners. We know it's because they never wondered who was behind the darkened windows of cars or learned to walk with keys pinched between their fingers like talons. We knew even before the zombies came a year ago.

We were girls, and we were born ready for danger.

+

In Ms. Rubble's class, I am learning that Anything Can Be a Weapon. A globe. A number 2 pencil. A bookcase. A stapler. Uncut toenails. An expired EpiPen. A hooked earring. A severe enough smell.

I wonder if my dad, six months gone, would have survived his zombie attack if he had taken this class. If he would have known to use the gas nozzle to gouge out the zombie's eyes, the scrub brush to sweep the zombie's clumsy feet out from under it. I don't share my thoughts with Ms. Rubble or my class. A sure sign that someone's about to fall prey to a zombie is that they start reminiscing about those they've lost. The First Rule in Anything Can Be a Weapon is Don't Look Back. Actually, the first rule is, Aim For the Head, especially the center. The brain is said to be soft in zombies. It is said to be the weak spot. I imagine a red and white bullseye. I imagine it like an egg exploding on the roof of a car. Ms. Rubble says using figurative language to describe our experiences is useful, psychologically. Similes, she says, were invented to help us see the beauty in violence.

+

Ms. Rubble is small and solid. Her calf muscles like cantaloupes, her biceps showing through her thick-knit cardigan. She wears tennis shoes and cargo shorts with her work blouses. She used to be a gymnast. We've seen a video of her twenty years younger, cracking her ankle on a dismount and not flinching, even a little.

At the end of her lesson, Ms. Rubble sits cross-legged on her desk, checks her watch, and announces, "Put away your notebooks, class. It's Drill day."

Every month, we have one scheduled Zombie Drill. During Zombie Drills, everyone is assigned a role, and every month our rolls switch. Last month I was Tactical, a window-boarder. The month before I was a Fighter. This month I'm a Survivor, which is a kind way of saying I'm a hider. Ms. Rubble is teaching me how to fold my body over itself, to become less than what I am.

"Like a scorpion," she told me. "The Ancient Romans believed scorpions would spontaneously generate from a pile of rags and hot bricks, because they'd show up in rooms people thought were impenetrable. They even found scorpions in the tombs with the Terracotta soldiers. Scorpions know how to flatten themselves." And then she bent her body impossibly and my joints ached as I mimicked.

All month, I've been stretching in bed before I sleep. Reaching my forehead for my ankles. I stretch in the shower and let the water run down my neck into my eyes. I feel my body go elastic. If I wanted to, I could fit myself into the ring of a tractor tire. I could angle my way into a file cabinet. I could cling to the bottom side of a bleacher for twenty-two minutes. If I let the air out of my lungs I could curl my limbs into the bottom of a janitor's yellow mop bucket. I understand the burrowing instinct. I felt it six months ago, curling under the dashboard of my dad's car, pulling my arms inside my sleeves towards the torso of my shirt, making myself as small as possible. I felt it as I crawled over the back of the seat into the trunk, squeezed my eyes shut, and imagined my body away.

"Hurry, class," Ms. Rubble says. "The alarm is supposed to go off at 10:25. Remember, you won't always be prepared for a Zombie attack. Concentrate on what you're doing. Memorize the steps so deep they're screwed in your muscles."

Most of the class reaches for objects that could be used as weapons. The quickest students get the protractors and staplers. The slower students are left with rulers and dictionaries. They circle the door, some face the windows.

I push pass them to the blue recycling bin next to the door and begin pressing the air from my lungs. I imagine the empty spaces in my body collapsing in on themselves, my body becoming compact. I fold myself into the bin, my ankles up by my ears, my chin tucked into my chest. I pull papers and plastic water bottles over myself, hiding my skin.

When the sirens begin to scream, Ms. Rubble shuts off the lights. It's dark for a very long time. Then someone kicks the door. One of my classmates, one of the fighters, screams, and I hear a yardstick drop to the floor.

"Sorry," she whispers, but no one responds. The door to the classroom is rattling on its hinges. This has never happened before. I know it's probably the teachers, testing to see how we'll act under pressure, but it doesn't feel fake. I think, *Maybe the Zombies ambushed the principal while he was activating the outdoor alarm. Maybe. Maybe. Maybe.* The window-boarders stack more desks in front of the door—I hear the legs screeching against the tiles—but still the door shakes. I feel my body tensing, my muscles contracting, my limbs threatening to spring back into its regular shape. I grip my ankles, bite down on my thigh.

Finally, the door stops shaking. The alarm goes off, and Ms. Rubble turns on the lights.

"New Rule," she says. "Never Scream."

+

A year ago, we were a Catholic school for girls. We learned about the insides of cells. We learned about how to measure a flag pole without even having to climb it. We ate lunch in a cafeteria with open doors and Windexed windows reading notes our parents tucked in our lunchboxes. Now, we only go home on weekends, because it's too dangerous to make the journey every day. We use up the superglue gluing the windows shut. We have classes called "Close Combat," and "Disinfect-It!" We sleep in bunks in the gymnasium, which has been sectioned into rooms by standing blackboards. We hoard chalk, use it to scratch fake windows with fake views of the ocean. We miss sunlight. We don't have recess anymore. We can never actually tell if it's nighttime or if all the bulbs have just been screwed out. At home our mothers are using power drills to install fourth and fifth pad locks to the doors. They are laying quiltwork against the windowpanes and plywood over that. They are using the phone-tree system from former Girl Scout troops to exchange tallies on canned goods and bottled water, and to pass around a self-defense DVD from the late 80's called "Bullshido," which is basically a series of clips of women being attacked from behind, jabbing their assailants, and then cutting to a jaunty blond in a shiny blue leotard who smiles and punch-kicks the air.

+

One thing that hasn't changed is we still learn about Greek myths. All of us want to be Artemis, who swore never to marry. In some stories, she is a life-giver. She helps women give birth on beds of green moss and makes fauns sprout from under stones like saplings. In some stories, she is a huntress. She bloodied men with arrows carved from cypress, she set traps in streams, slipped pincher bugs into beds. Our history teacher told us some scholars believed Artemis's namesake was *artemes*, meaning "safe," while others believed it to be linked to *artamos*: "butcher." We like a woman who could be both, like us.

+

The night of the Drill, my bunkmate and I can't sleep.

Zumi is a fighter this month. She tells me, "When the door started shaking, I wanted it to be real. I wanted to fuck those fuckers up." She laughs. "With a yardstick."

Zumi has never been face to face with a Zombie. Like most of the girls here, she's just seen them from a distance, milling through abandoned mall parking lots or stumbling by the side of the road. Most people don't know how close I've gotten. They don't know that I was there when the Zombies came for my Dad, don't know that instead of fighting I hid. I made myself disappear. They don't know that when given the chance to Fight, to Protect, I chose to be a Survivor.

"Do you notice?" Zumi says, "The government doesn't call them Zombies, even though that's what they are. They call them Sick. It's like no one wants to admit what's happening."

The Zombies who attacked my father were sallow, ribs showing. Zombies, I know, will eat anything. The air from their lungs carries sickness. At first, hospitals sent them to mental wards. Sometimes they behaved, and other times they'd be talking to people who weren't there, or tried plucking out their own eyelashes, or would hiss at the hot water from a shower. Then they got feral. They gnawed on railings like animals. They bent their ears down until they warped. Their eyes turned rose-colored; their hair fell out in clots. Their arms swelled. They scratched and bit and body-slammed and drew blood. It almost sounded pretty when you said it like that – 'drew blood' – as though our Dads were all in art class, not the rich and fenceless night.

+

Sometimes I worry I'm becoming one of them. There are nights I wake up in a cold sweat, fingers tingling, lips numb. Sometimes during class, my lungs turn to lead and I feel a pressure behind my eyes like I might cry. I have to run to the bathroom and lean my forehead against the mirror, do pull-ups in a stall until the feeling goes away. I have thoughts that won't leave me, that get lodged in my brain like the skin around popcorn gets stuck in my gums. I think about things that happened a long time ago, things I haven't thought about in years, things that now turn me nauseous with guilt: the time a boy I knew said he wanted to stab himself and I never told anyone about it, the time a hungry dog came up to me and I kicked it, *hard*, the time I wrote my name against a glass window to see if my Zombie-Dad would recognize it, and my mother snatched me from the window and slammed the shutters, but not before I saw movement behind the trees.

A couple months ago, I asked my mother about my Dad. She was going through the toolbox looking for a pocket-sized wrench for me to carry. She already had me keep a box-cutter in my bedroom, thumbtacks in a Tic Tac container, a nail-file in my shoe.

"What would you do if you saw him?" I asked.

"It wouldn't be your dad anymore, sweetie," she replied. Hovering over the toolbox, her hair covered her face.

"But what would you do?"

Her hands stopped moving, stopped searching. She turned to face me. "Baby. I'd shoot him."

And that was the end of the conversation.

I envy Zumi on the top bunk. I envy that she doesn't know what she'd do when she finally does face a Zombie. I envy her for still thinking she'd be brave.

+

I enroll in a class called "How to Tell if Your Loved One is Becoming a Zombie." I say it's fulfilling a pre-rec. I say my course load's pretty full this spring and I just want something breezy. I don't tell anyone about how I've started to pick at the hairs around my temples and lay at night for hours staring at the door to the gym, wondering what it'd be like to just leave.

The class is held in the old speech-pathologist's room, which I guess is really an office. There are only 5 of us enrolled in "How to Tell." We all crowd around a kidney-shaped desk with our teacher, the head of the kidney.

Our teacher used to be the school psychiatrist, and I'm not unconvinced she's leading this class to suss out zombie sympathizers or those showing the pre-existing conditions. Her nails are long and untrimmed, a habit of many of our teachers, and I can see hers are sharpened at the tips, detailed with a single tear-drop shape in red. She wears large geometric rings on most of her fingers. Her hair is so short her ears stick out. I can smell her breath. She wears jeans and carries one of those hammers that holds about 4 screwdrivers inside. I like her instantly. I'm nervous instantly. She reminds me of a wolf.

She doesn't introduce herself. Instead, she gives a lecture on the Z-strain as she augments the lid of a green bean can into a throwing star with her pocketknife.

"There are times you wouldn't even know you've been infected. When you kiss someone. When you share a toothbrush. When you eat something unwashed or unsealed."

I'm thinking of a peeled banana that was passed around the bunks one night. At least six of us girls shared it. I tried to remember if I was the first one to take a bite or the last. I'm thinking of the time in the bathroom not too long ago, when Megan and Louisa touched tongues on a dare.

"You know someone's a zombie when their wounds don't

bother them."

"You know someone's a zombie when their fever spikes through the roof of their head and they feel like fainting but instead of fainting they die and reanimate."

She sets her throwing-star down on the table and spins it in place.

"How do you know what being a zombie feels like?" asks Kay.

I am wondering the same thing too. I am wondering, *Does anyone who becomes a zombie ever come back?* The teacher doesn't answer. Instead, she throws her throwing-star into a bulletin board. It quivers.

That night I take the nail filer out of my shoe. I hold it in my right hand, and I scrape the knuckles of my left hand across the blade. It hurts bad, but not so bad I can't handle it. I hold my skin to my mouth and suck at the wound. My blood tastes like salt.

+

Ms. Rubble recruits the strongest of us to go on a real Zombie Raid. She says that some of us are ready, that we have nothing more to learn from fake fighting, from throwing punches at the air. Zumi gets chosen first, and I'm surprised when Ms. Rubble also calls my name next. "But I've been a Survivor this month," I say, and she responds, "You were a Fighter three months ago. You know how to be cautious. And you're quick. We need that."

This is the first time anyone in our class has been chosen for a Zombie Raid. Usually it's older girls. They leave scared and come back bruised, swaggering, high-fiving. Zumi has heard that the teachers only take students to zombie packs they know are slow, easy first kills to build our confidence.

But you never know what will happen for sure. Rumor is last month, a girl went missing on a Raid.

Ms. Rubble gives us old police riot gear that's too big for us but makes us feel impenetrable and strong. We wear helmets with opaque lids. We wear flame retardant gloves. There are five of us in total. Ms. Rubble encourages us make a pact that we keep going, even if one of us falls. I agree, even though I'm not confident that I can stick to it, because I want to be seen as brave. I want to be someone who can be counted on.

"Kill me if you have to," Zumi whispers to me.

We shake hands through our riot gear, our firefighter gear, our hazmat suits, our gloves and goggles and boots.

"We're starting you off easy," Ms. Rubble says as she leads us through the teacher's lounge, a school exit we didn't even know about. To a fenced yard we didn't know about. "We found these guys roaming around the old playground last night and rounded them up for you."

In the yard: twin apple trees, and tied to them, the zombies.

A collection of three beat-up-looking ones, collared and chained. They kind of look like dads. Hawaiian polos. Birkenstocks. Cargo shorts. One in a ball-cap. One with grass stains. One with Ladies Man emblazoned on his shirt.

One's my dad.

Ms. Rubble cocks a Taser and says, "They'll be released one at a time. You are graded on agility, team-work, evasion, and effectiveness. Your goal is to disable – knock 'em out. If you are wounded, you will be sent into quarantine. If he breaks skin, you will be thrown over the wall." A stopwatch hangs from her neck. My dad bats at the sunlight like it's fruit flies. He's purple-blue with bruises. His wedding ring's still on.

But some other zombie, not my dad, gets released at the click of the button. The zombie stumbles forward, glaring, moaning, absently rubbing one arm. He doesn't look like a monster yet, but we've learned about this. We call it the warm-up stage. He stretches the muscles in his neck. Curls and uncurls his hands. Works his jaw. My knees bend automatically. I see a baseball bat leaning against the tree. Zumi's faster though, is already behind the zombie right as he's starting to crouch, like he can leap across the yard teeth-bared, into our throats.

Zumi has strong arms, used to play softball. It takes one swing.

My dad is pulling against his chains now, riled by the action. I wonder if all of these zombies are dads of the students chosen. Is that the real test? To see if we'll hesitate?

The Ladies Man zombie is released next. His eyes, despite being half out of their sockets, are focused on me. I feel a jolt of electricity in my chest. "Go!" Zumi yells.

I get a running start and slide-kick his feet out from under him. As he falls, I catch the chain still swinging from his wrist. It's a risky move, intentionally going to the ground, but I feel reckless. Even now, I know that part of me wants to be hurt, wants to be removed from the game before I have to make a choice. I spring to my feet, place a foot on Ladies Man's back, wrap the chain around his neck, and pull tight.

Even as I decapitate the zombie, I can't stop picturing that moment in Dad's car. When I shrunk into nothing in the trunk. When I heard the glass shatter and my dad struggle, the way the car rocked and my dad slammed the door shut on what sounded like an arm or a leg – slamming and slamming while I lay still inside it, tiny as a kidney stone. I always imagined he'd been bit on the neck but now I see it was his hands, both hands. How he must have held someone's teeth open like a bear trap ready to spring.

He's the next one to be released. My dad. But not really my dad.

"Take him," Ms. Rubble screams.

He stumbles forward, and I tell myself that there is nothing familiar in his movements. If he looks the way he did shuffling into the kitchen every morning, back still sore from sleep, it's only because our brains are wired to find familiar in the unfamiliar. Our brains turn clouds into castles, cliff walls into faces. I think about letting my dad bite me. How poetically tragic that would be. Maybe in the moment his teeth unlatched from my skin, I'd see a glimmer of recognition in his eyes. His eyebrows would soften. Maybe as my brain softened, I'd discover a secret zombie language, and I'd be able to talk to him again.

But then, Dad lurches at me. Teeth-bared, lips curled. And I know this is never a face my father would make. I jump out of the way, then kick into the crook behind his knees. It doesn't feel like I'm kicking my dad. It doesn't feel like the time I kicked that stray dog.

Another girl jumps in, slams him across the face with a piece of plywood. My dad gurgles and twitches on the ground.

"Again," I tell her, and she brings the wood down hard enough that his face starts to flatten. He's not moving anymore, but I want her to keep going. I want to stand here and watch her hit until the skull cracks and no part of this zombie looks like my dad anymore.

But then I feel Ms. Rubble's hand on the back of my neck, the only part of me not covered. "Good girl," she says. "Now time to stand down."

+

With all the zombie-dads destroyed, Ms. Rubble leads us into the forest beyond the school. She tells us a pack of zombies have been spotted stalking an apartment complex nearby. We're going to take them out.

My limbs feel warm and ready. I feel patches of fern and moss bend under my feet. A woodpecker knocks on a hollow tree somewhere close by.

I can already feel it. The next time we meet a zombie, it'll be exactly like TV. It'll be exactly a videogame. I'll almost be able to see an outline of white and the choices hovering above them: Strangle. Subdue. A shovel will feel natural; a gun will feel good. When I move to kill a zombie, it'll be like some switch in the back of my neck has been touched. It will be as if I've been always killing zombies.

Unit 3: Pop Quiz

Below is a cross-section of your brain. Label its parts.

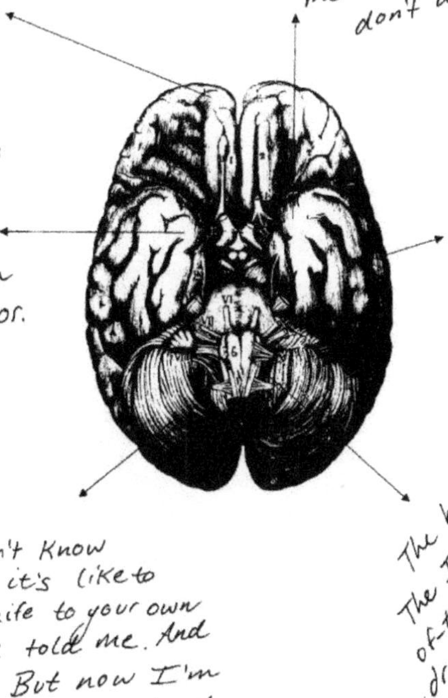

I think this is
where all the repressed
memories are. I
don't want to
know.

My friend's
blood on
my knuckles.
Her tooth
on the floor.

"You don't know
what it's like to
hold a knife to your own
throat," he told me. And
I didn't. But now I'm
starting to understand.

The buffet dream.
The I'm-at-the-end-
of-the-buffet-line
dream. So many
options, and I'm
afraid I'll miss
my chance
to choose.

THE FLOATING AWAY SCHOOL

"Calm down," the teacher says when the lights flicker out and the projectors darken. "Everything's fine, relax," she tells us, as the earth rumbles and we feel the school tip. "There is no need for anyone to be standing up," she barks, even though our desks are sliding slantwise towards the windows. Our trapper keepers do cartwheels. Ramona covers her mouth, is going to be sick. But our teacher, Ms. G, is steady as a barbell. She is a physicist. A horseback rider. No stranger to momentum. When something scrapes against the side of our building, she pushes though the desks and chairs and our tiny human bodies, hoisting the blinds so our classroom fills with sunshine. She takes a good long look outside.

We look too, ignoring her directions to stay seated and pressing our faces flat against the windowpanes.

What we see is the tops of trees. What we see is our neighborhood shrinking. Our school seems ripped from the earth, pipes and cables trailing behind us like roots. Outside our window we still have the edge of a sidewalk, half our playground with a jagged drop at one end, and a bicycle teetering over the edge and then back towards us, trying hard not to fall.

We float over the city streets, over midday traffic clogging Broadway. We float over a bowling alley and a baseball diamond and a crematorium and a carwash. The buildings are getting smaller. Soon we won't be able to recognize them for what they are.

"Is this supposed to happen?" asks Justice, looking back over his shoulder, hands knuckled on the window's edge.

Ms. G chews her lips and decides to say, "This is a scientific opportunity. The hypothesis is our school is floating away. Now, let's observe. What do you notice?"

The school lurches. Some of us scream.

She gets the word "blue" out of us. "Sky." "Clouds."

"Go on," she says. She's steady in her flat-bottomed sneakers and her practical, black skirt. We're inching higher slowly, slowly. It's like what we imagined being in a hot air balloon would feel like, except without the comforting puff of flames, the warm smell of the hand-woven basket.

"We see a little town below us."

"That little town is our town," she reminds us kindly. "It only seems small because of perspective."

"Traffic."

"A squad of police cars."

"Excellent," she says. "What else?"

"Well, Ms. G," says Annabelle, pushing a braid over one shoulder. Her hands shake, so she stuffs them in her pockets. "I can see part of the playground has torn away. But we still have one swing." Out the window, it's the one part of the playground still attached to our little scrap of school land.

"It's yellow. It moves in the wind," says Euphoria.

"Moves?" prompts Ms. G. "Can we think of a stronger word than 'moves'?"

"Twirls? Spins? Swings? Flails?"

"I like 'flails' best," explains Ms. G, "since it lets us know the fierceness of the wind."

And it's true, glancing outside, we can see the swing twisting uncontrollably. How fast are we traveling? How high are we getting? Is someone steering us, or are we at the whim of the wind currents, like a hot-air balloon?

This is what we wonder as Ms. G shoves open the windows so we can use our other senses: smell and touch, our faces pressed against the mesh of the screen.

"It's cooler out here," we say, surprised by the sharp wind, by the hairs on our arms extending.

"And what else?" she asks, poking a barometer into the wind.

"I'm touching a cloud," says Juan Pablo. "Whoa."

"Describe the cloud. What does a cloud feel like?"

"Like a wet lamb!"

"Like a cotton swab!"

"Marvelous!" cries Ms. G, scribbling beautifully on the white board. We love her for the way she can write in cursive without even looking, her marker to the board, her face to us. "What else do you notice?"

"Mountains. Um...pointy?...mountains." They loom far away on the horizon. They make a fence between us and the sky.

"Good," she says. "Anything else?"

"Helicopters."

"And could you give me a more detailed description please?"

"The chop-chop-chop of the helicopters, helicopter-sized, outside our windows."

"And men."

"Like, a lot of them."

They have headsets and goggles, and point to us, mouths moving, not knowing what to say.

+

I take the men in helicopters as a good sign. They rappel

carefully to the jagged edge of playground, anchor themselves to the post holding the swing. "That swing's a death trap," one of them says. He has a radio strapped to his shoulder, long sideburns, a knife Velcroed to his chest. He cuts the swing free and it flies off somewhere. Back down to earth. I imagine it crash-landing in some lady's swimming pool, her dog dragging it inside like a dead bird. Then he maneuvers towards our windows, squeezes into our Science classroom.

He's shiny and bulky and brought a duffle bag full of sandwiches, and the only one who can't eat them is Ramona, because she's allergic to raspberry jam.

"Some nice women at St. Anne's set to making them as soon as they saw you float away," he says to her. Ramona stalks off to the far corner near the door and sits with a sweater over her face as the rest of us nibble our food curiously. The sun is setting. Technically, we're still at school. We chew around the crusts while the man hands Ms. G an electric lantern, a case of protein bars to last days, an emergency radio, shows her the switches to flip, gives her a little manual on Morse Code "in case." He keeps saying "in case" and "we wouldn't want to upset the children" and he keeps counting us over and over like we are a flock of sacred sheep.

He drops a duffle of army-issue blankets. "No pillows," he grunts, and we start to wonder if Ms. G will make us sleep sitting-up, in STAR position, our hands folded in front of us on our desks. We haven't been allowed to leave the classroom, even to use the bathroom, and we begin to wonder how our friends in other classrooms are faring. We wonder if they got dessert with their sandwiches. Some of us have little sisters or brothers.

"Um," Ms. G whispers, but we are adept at teacher

whispering. "I have a dog back in my apartment. I'm growing...concerned."

The man with the sideburns, with the shiny muscles, says something about atmospheric forces. Something about how they can't remove any students or teachers from the school at this time. "A slight decrease in weight," he says, "might send your school soaring toward the stratosphere. And no one wants that.

"Can I give you my address? There's a key hidden in the planter." She's already written it out on a post-it note, a real pro of a teacher. She hasn't even opened her peanut butter and raspberry jam sandwich yet, is looking the man dead-on in the eyes like she does when she knows someone's cheating. He takes the paper from her, but he doesn't really answer her, doesn't even nod, just slips back out the window without so much as a "yes."

+

Everything's fine for a couple of days. Now that we're at cloud level, we don't seem to be rising or falling. Ms. G is extra nice to us, gives us leisurely breaks, lets us lie on our backs while she reads, lets us close our eyes, comb each other's hair with our fingers. She lets us push our desks against the walls, lets us stomp our feet and holler, teaches us to stretch, teaches us to sleep back to back so we're comfortable. We eat protein bars and stale sandwiches during our regular snack breaks. We stop remembering to be afraid. The school is a kingdom now—not much, but ours.

Twice a day we take observations, try to identify the clouds and what they mean. Today, they make a ceiling over us and a floor below us. There's a storm bubbling out there. Rain patters across the rooftop and streaks down the windows. We count the seconds between a lightning and its thunder. Ms. G leads us through the scientific process: we create a hypothesis to answer the question: how will we be rescued?

We think: a flock of birds picks us up and takes us to our parents.

We think: airplanes will sidle up and scoop us out.

We think: we'll crash into a mountain, and we'll be saved by mountain men.

When the storm is all around us, it's much louder, it's banging, like softballs, it cracks a window, darkens around us, we scream – but it passes. When the clouds clear we realize we're not just floating, but moving. The pointy mountains we'd seen on the first day are closer than they were before. The school is taking us to them.

+

The helicopters come again on day five. Ms. G is livid with the men when they arrive. Ms. G uses her I-*saw*-you-put-gum-in-that-girl's-hair look that sends us hiding under our desks.

"It's been almost a week, and we're still here. We've almost finished the cell biology unit, and we weren't supposed to get to that lesson until April."

The man takes her by the arm and whispers in her ear. He gestures to us. He's speaking quietly enough that we can't catch the words, but we think we can imagine what he's saying, "You understand, miss," or "There's nothing we can do."

Ms. G tries harder, switches tones, says, "Please, my sister is in the hospital," says, "I need to renew my auto insurance," says, "I think I have Jury Duty today – is it the

18th? Sir, you need to take me down."

But the man just hands her sandwiches and dried shampoo and tic-tacs and a hairbrush, delivers a load of hand-knit sweaters that some concerned troupe of grandmothers made for the poor schoolchildren-who-floated-away. He climbs out the window.

"How long are we expected to just stay up here like this?" she calls to him, indignant, still in her sneakers, her skirt covered in shed hairs and pencil shavings, her hair pinned back fiercely. As she says this, a helicopter swoops down to pick him up, and maybe he doesn't hear her, or maybe he chooses not to. The helicopter hovers above the schoolyard, not wanting to disrupt the equilibrium, not wanting us to tip. The lights swing back and forth, blinding us, emptying the shadowed corners of the room. The man climbs in, and the helicopter takes off. I think, if he couldn't take us, maybe he could have taken letters to loved ones, to families. I think too late of my parents down there, in a square roof-shaped box. The further we drift, the closer to the mountains we float, the less they feel my own.

+

When the helicopters don't return, we try calling them on the radios, but all we get is static. We're almost out of protein bars, and the hungriest of us chew down pencils and grind our molars against the wooden rulers. Ms. G pulls the plastic wrapping off of unopened stacks of paper and hangs it outside the windows to collect dew. She says we can go weeks without food, as long as we have water.

One night it storms. Ms. G pulls down the blinds to block out the lightning, but still we can hear it. We lean into each others' backs and wonder if we can pretend ourselves into sleep. When the storm is over, it's nearly dawn, and there are apples. Apples all over the half-playground. Red and perfect and ours.

We wait for Ms. G to explain it. We wait for her to demand we hypothesize, but she can just stare.

"Go," she says.

Ms. G allows the smallest and fastest of us to climb out the window and into the wet grass to gather the fruits. We're afraid it's a trick at first, that she might change her mind at the last moment and we'll be banned from games for the day, but she nods us forward. The smallest and the fastest is me, but I take my time. It's the first time I've left the classroom in days, and I walk barefoot through the grass that's grown as high as my ankles.

I eat an apple from the ground. It's sour and delicious. Its skin is as cool as the sky.

+

The storms keep coming. The storms keep bringing us things: a monsoon of toothbrushes, a drizzle of Nutragrain bars, a blizzard of celery and carrots. "The sky is our mother now!" Justice decides. Because it's true, we never go hungry. Ms. G isn't in charge any more than we are. We just keep moving towards those mountains that used to be scenery and are now almost foreground, closer, coming in.

One day Ms. G says, "To hell with it," and swings open our classroom door. At first, we're afraid of the structural integrity of the hallway, afraid the school will suddenly tilt and propel us through the halls like a loogie shooting out of a straw. But the promise of movement, of sliding in our socks down the shiny, waxed floor, makes us brave. We peer into other classrooms, the empty desks, the janitor's closet locked tight.

We return to our classroom only to climb out the windows into the playground. As our feet land on grass, and then blacktop, a flock of butterflies descends on us, swirls around our building like a tornado. There are thousands of them. I've never seen so many butterflies. Ms. G joins us on the playground. The wind whips her hair out of its pins, and she sits cross-legged on the end of the slide. She tells us a group of butterflies is called a "kaleidoscope," a "rabble," a "swarm," but we like "kaleidoscope" best, the way monarchs and blue morphos and Goliath birdwings and mourning cloaks and peacock butterflies and postmans and red admirals and summer Azores and tiger swallowtails and all the other butterflies not listed in our science books swirl – like tiny construction paper triangles – like the recycle bin from art class got dumped – except these are wings and legs, not paper and glue, these are landing on the lawn and taking off like thoughtlessness.

+

It's been three weeks. We still find the crushed wings of the butterflies in our windows, in our hair, under our shoes. We've had two Saturdays in the sky. It rained meatballs, seriously, *meatballs,* just like the book. We can't stop laughing. It rained celery sticks, it rained warm soup. We're higher than the houses, lower than the airplanes. The mountains are close enough for us to see shadows from clouds moving across them, but not close enough to know if we'll be able to clear the peaks or if we'll crash into them. The air up here is thin, cool. Even when we take deep breaths, it feels like breathing through a straw. It reminds us of health class, how the teacher would have us try breathing through straws the size of coffee stirrers and say, "This is what smokers feel." But this airlessness is different. It makes us euphoric, light.

We catch Ms. G on the lawn one morning, the lawn outside our classroom windows, the lawn where the earth cracked apart before we floated away. She is crawling on her knees, grabbing the grass in fistfuls. Maybe she's pretending to be her horse, the horse she used to ride on desert trails, the horse she must miss. She stands, staggering, trying not to lose her bearings. It starts raining shampoo. It is soapy and rainbow like the suds in car washes. Rainbows form in the sheen of the bubbles. She stands there soaking, her skirt billowing, her hair a flag.

When she crawls back inside, we see that her eyes are red.

"Class," she says. "I just don't know anymore."

She drips suds onto the floor, and we move so that they don't touch us.

+

All this time the power's been out, but we learn how to make contact with nearby radio towers by tuning our radios into the right frequency. The messages are mostly for us. We say the things that pilots say, like, "We're cruising at a steady altitude of 30,000 feet" or "We apologize to any students who experience turbulence" or "A message to our students this morning: your parents love you very much." Sometimes a voice responds to us, once a loud shock jock trying to get callers on the line to ask us questions, once a woman from NPR who reads to us is a voice soft as grass, but usually it's just us, then static.

Even though we have more freedom than ever—we can

roam the whole school, sleep or play or wander the playground whenever we want—we grow anxious, we grow bored, tired of the empty space that contains us. We return to our abandoned hypotheses. This time, our guiding question is how do we save ourselves. We learned constellations and recorded barometrics and deconstructed tables and hypothesized and made predictions and prototypes on the whiteboard of the aircraft that we will make to save us. Of the wings we will glue to our arms. Of the ropes we braid together so they will not break.

"Can't we just turn the tables into a plane?" we ask Ms. G.

"Do we have anything to make a rocket, a jetpack, something soft to land on?"

Ms. G has stopped teaching, stopping asking us to analyze and observe. But she's been measuring our desks and tables with a meter stick. She's been scratching at the walls at night. She's been smoking by the windows. Cigarettes we didn't even know she had. We're not used to teachers being this way.

Ms. G asks us if we want to learn how to smoke, and of course we all say yes. It's all about the inhale, she says, and we practice, choking. Tyler's being a real sissy about it, says it causes cancer, but those of us with Ms. G don't give a shit. She taught us the word shit. She's been writing curse words on the board, showing us how to spit them out.

"Hell, let's go outside. Let's look over the edge," she says, so we do.

We link hands but not because we're told to. We walk to the end of the playground, where blacktop turns to crumbling dirt. We can feel the unsteadiness of the ground underneath us. It's just a thin crust. It sounds like it's cracking.

"What if we fall," asks Melody.

"Then we die," says Ms. G.

We walk to the edge of the earth together, our hair blowing back, our legs shaking, the foundation whining. There are shelf clouds on the horizon. And there are the mountains right in front of us. After all these weeks of watching them grow closer, now we could reach out and grab them by the trees. I can't believe how beautiful it is. The smell is evergreen and earthy. We reach out and touch the mountain—the soft tips of evergreen, a flock of crows, a dry squirrel nest. It's not just that we're Ms. G's class anymore. We are the whole damn school. Reaching over the edge, our fingertips brush the tips of trees, the first anchored thing we've touched since the school shook loose.

"What mountain range is this?" Annabelle asks. "What is our elevation above sea level?"

Ms. G shushes her. For weeks we took data, tested hypotheses, ruminated over cloud charts. Now it's time to observe without naming.

The ground under us tilts. Our floating school is tilting under the weight of all us convened in one place. We dig our heels into the dirt. Those of us with our feet still in lawn grab fistfuls of grass in one hand and the backs of classmates' T-shirts with the other. We lean toward and away from the mountain at the same time.

Ms. G says "Let go," and she sounds like herself again. She's telling us to jump like she has told us to study, to double-check our answers, to wash our hands before lunch. And we try to, we do, but we've spent our whole lives learning not to fall.

"This is my job," Ms. G says. "To help you let go."

We are all afraid, but one voice says, "I have to, I can't take it," and he leaps from our floating school to the mountain top.

We pitch on our floating school. We rise just enough to notice the difference. We can still touch the trees, but just barely. We realize: we either all jump now, or those of us left will float higher, get further from the earth. This might be our last chance – and that feeling descends on us, soundless and simple as snow.

Ramona jumps next. We see her land, miraculously, in an eagle's nest. She waves at us. We rise just a little bit more. Tyler jumps next, then Juan Pablo. Katherine and Danica grab hands and leap into a patch of oak trees. Justice jumps. Then I do, my legs pinwheeling. I fall into a pine tree and hug its needled branches, the trunk bending against my weight but not breaking. I look up. With every person who leaves, the school loses a little bit of what's holding it back and rises higher into the sky. Soon, the school will be too high for anyone else to survive the jump onto the mountain.

Ms. G stays on the cracked edge of the playground. She sits. Her feet dangle over the edge.

"What are you doing, Ms. G?" we ask.

"Come with us!"

"You never taught us how wolves evolved into whales. Or why time moves slower in outer space than it does here."

"We don't know the way home," we say.

We can see the bottoms of her feet now. "You guys look beautiful," she tells us. "You guys. This is my job."

We swing from treetops, sap staining our hands, and we yell up to her, "What about Jury Duty? What about your cat? Or was it a dog?"

Up, up the school goes. From the bottom, it's a nest of dirt and roots and wires. We watch it float over the mountain and sail out of sight on breezes we can't see.

+

Some days I still think about the school, if she's still up there. When we climbed down our trees to the mountain floor, we counted ourselves again and again. Can she really be alone? Maybe she unknits our sweaters. Reknits our sweaters. If she can make a big enough parachute, we think, she can make it back to earth.

Maybe she finds land higher than our mountaintop. Maybe she lands in Egypt, starts a new life balanced on the tippy top of the Great Pyramid.

Maybe she drifts over Everest, nabs a victory flag from an American climber, wears it like a cape.

Maybe she's pulled into the Bermuda Triangle and finds Amelia Earhart drinking tea on a cloud.

Maybe she lassoes flocks of migrating geese and harnesses them like a pack of sled dogs.

Those of us who jumped have a lot of time to wonder. It takes us three days to hike down the mountain. Our feet move slowly on an earth that is too big for us to feel its movement. We chew on pine needles to trick our hunger. We ask each other, "Do you think she'll survive?" and "Why didn't she jump?" We wonder if the more interesting question is "Why did we?"

None of us can see the school anymore, even when we climb to the top of the tallest trees.

At night, the stars overtake us.

We think it's most likely she kept gaining altitude, passed through the layers of the sky one by one until she breached the exosphere. So when Ms. G looks out the window all she sees is blackness, all she sees is space.

ACKNOWLEDGMENTS

Thank you to the journals where these stories first appeared and to the editors who published them (in slightly different forms): *The Adroit Journal, Squalorly Lit, Necessary Fiction, The Offing, Sundog Lit, Indianola Review, Passages North, Heavy Feather Review,* and *Moon City Press*. A special thanks to the editors at *Passages North*, who serendipitously published both the first and last story we wrote for this collection. We think that's neat! Thank you to Anne Valente, for choosing our story for the Waasnode Fiction Prize for *Passages North* and for saying such nice things about "The Boy Who Arrives in a Box."

Thank you to our brilliant Gold Wake editors Nick Courtright, Kyle McCord, and Rachel Geffrey. You approached us with incredible support, respect, insight, and thoughtfulness. Truly, you have made this book better, on micro and macro scales.

Thank to Andrea Ucini for our gorgeous cover art. We love it!

And, it bears repeating, thank you to all our teachers. Thank you especially, Susquehanna and the Writing Program. Because we met there, took classes together, spent a summer subletting an apartment and binging *The Last Airbender* together. Susquehanna was where we co-edited the *The Susquehanna University Review* and had the privilege of learning from our phenomenal, brilliant professors. Thank you, Gary Fincke, Glen Retief, Tom Bailey, Joseph Scapellato, Silas Zobal, Karla Kelsey, and especially Catherine Dent, who mentored both of us and who we both love dearly. We really do, Catherine. DEARLY.

To our students who we've ever told are writers. Keep writing.

To our Adroit Summer mentees. Keep writing.

To our amazing partners, who keep our hearts afloat, and who we will gush about in due time. Also, thanks to our animal pals, Oliver P. Rabbit (Bun Bun) and Anjelica Huston (Angie) who have the honor of getting their full names published in this collection. You are the true heroes.

From Dana

I've spent the majority of my life in schools, as either a student or as a teacher. Some of the most important moments of my life have happened in classrooms, in band rooms, on the sidewalks crisscrossing a campus. I wouldn't be who I am without these physical spaces. So, thank you to Becht Elementary, with its creaky hardwood floors and cracked, brick walls (good to hide injured moths in). Thank you to Four Mile Elementary with its playground bordered by the woods (that I always wanted to enter but never did). Thank you to Loyalsock Middle School and High School. Thank you to Arizona State University, and most of all thank you to Susquehanna University, where Melissa and I first met.

Thank you to my teachers and peers who transformed classrooms into magical places. Thank you to Mrs. Krout and Mrs. Kastner for telling me I was a writer and for helping me to believe it. Thank you to my wonderful, talented mentors from Arizona State University: Tara Ison, Melissa Pritchard,

Peter Turchi, Matt Bell, and T.M. McNally. You made this hot, desert place a home.

Thank you to all of my students who one day might flip through this book and think, "Hey, that's me!"

Thank you to my Tucson friends with their dogs and witchiness and board games and pool toys and fine teas. Thank you to the Housemates, who I wish could be my housemates forever. Thank you to my mom and dad and brother for loving me and supporting me endlessly.

Thank you to Will. The talented, tall, terrific Will. You bring so much happiness to my days.

Finally, thank you to Melissa. Thank you for being the biggest fan of my work, for finding joy in even my earliest, roughest drafts. Thank you for giving me a popsicle when I was stung by a bee in your pool. Thank you for helping our stories to run wild. I've learned so much from you, and you are truly the best.

From Melissa

I have always loved school, being in school, buying new notebooks and boxes of pens, writing the date in the top right corner in perfect script, got butterflies every August before I taught. I'm grateful for my elementary schools: Saint Michael's, with pine trees taller than the school and a field that went on forever; Martensdale St. Mary's, in the sticks; Sacred Heart, where I wore jeans with a chain once and felt cool. Thank you to my favorite childhood teachers, especially Mrs. Eller and Ms. Holsapple, who told me I was a writer, and Mr. Rohwer, who helped me hear music in everything.

Thank you to my former fourth grade students, for saying things like, "It's like the clocks have stopped working in their bodies," and for writing things like, "There should be truth in this poem. There's not." Thank you for being the best writers in the room.

Thank you, again, to Susquehanna University, my absolute favorite school.

Thank you to the University of Arizona MFA Program, my amazing peers, the incomparable Poetry Center (where I sometimes took the most exquisite poet-naps), and especially my teachers: Aurelie Sheehan, Manuel Muñoz, Joshua Marie Wilkinson, Ander Monson, Jane Miller, and Kate Bernheimer.

Thank you to my Tucson family, who have made me feel alive and enough in this desert. Thank you to all the Susquehanna-transplants, the ladies of Catan, Phoenix friends, to the Riverwalk and stars you can see inside the city. Thank you, wild rabbits and monsoon rain.

Special thanks to Mariah Young, the Ann Perkins of humans.

Thank you to faraway friends, my pen-pals and Twitter pals and SU pals and Bucknell poets and the friends I would answer the phone for in the middle of the night because I LOVE YOU GODDAMNIT and I can't stop.

Special thanks to Billie Tadros, you 110% human.

Thank you to my family, who never once said writing was a waste of time. Special thanks to Emory, who I love completely and who completely rules.

Thank you, Jeff, who I love with my whole damn heart. Thank you for your warmth, compassion, animal drawings, rabbit pics, jokes about ketchup fights, your excellent laugh, your unwavering support, and for tickling me while I was writing this sentence. You are my good place, and I am so grateful to share a life with you.

And Dana Diehl. THE DANA DIEHL. You are the best writer I know. You made every story in this collection better.

You grounded us, and humanized/humorized our stories. Thank you for fixing it when I put two spaces after a period. Thank you for listening to me. Not only are you this amazing writer, but one of the best humans I know. My dear and lovely friend, I love you. And I love writing with you.

ABOUT GOLD WAKE PRESS

Gold Wake Press, an independent publisher, is curated by Nick Courtright and Kyle McCord. All Gold Wake titles are available at amazon.com, barnesandnoble.com, and via order from your local bookstore. Learn more at goldwake.com.

Available Titles:

Brandon Amico's *Disappearing, Inc.*
Andy Briseño's *Down and Out*
Sarah Anne Strickley's *Fall Together*
Talia Bloch's *Inheritance*
Eileen G'Sell's *Life After Rugby*
Erin Stalcup's *Every Living Species*
Glenn Shaheen's *Carnivalia*
Frances Cannon's *The High and Lows of Shapeshift Ma and Big-Little Frank*
Justin Bigos' *Mad River*
Kelly Magee's *The Neighborhood*
Kyle Flak's *I Am Sorry for Everything in the Whole Entire Universe*
David Wojciechowski's *Dreams I Never Told You & Letters I Never Sent*
Keith Montesano's *Housefire Elegies*
Mary Quade's *Local Extinctions*

Adam Crittenden's *Blood Eagle*
Lesley Jenike's *Holy Island*
Mary Buchinger Bodwell's *Aerialist*
Becca J. R. Lachman's *Other Acreage*
Joshua Butts' *New to the Lost Coast*
Tasha Cotter's *Some Churches*
Hannah Stephenson's *In the Kettle, the Shriek*
Nick Courtright's *Let There Be Light*
Kyle McCord's *You Are Indeed an Elk, but This Is Not the Forest You Were Born to Graze*
Kathleen Rooney's *Robinson Alone*
Erin Elizabeth Smith's *The Naming of Strays*

ABOUT THE AUTHORS

Dana Diehl is the author of *Our Dreams Might Align* (Splice UK, 2018) and *TV Girls*, which was the winner of the 2017-2018 New Delta Review Chapbook Contest. She earned her MFA in Fiction at Arizona State University and her BA in Creative Writing at Susquehanna University. Her work has been published in *North American Review*, *Necessary Fiction*, *Passages North*, and elsewhere. She lives in Tucson.

Melissa Goodrich is the author of the story collection *Daughters of Monsters* and the poetry chapbook *IF YOU WHAT*. She earned her BA in Creative Writing from Susquehanna University and her MFA in Fiction from the University of Arizona. Her stories have appeared in *American Short Fiction, The Kenyon Review Online, Passages North, PANK*, and others, and her honors include the 2016 Tucson Festival of Books Fiction Award, the 2018 Passages North Waasnode Fiction Prize, the 2013 Margaret Sterling Memorial Award, the 2013 AWP Intro Award, and the 2012 Academy of American Poets Prize.